Air Fryer Cookbook for Beginners 2023

A Truly Healthy, Oil-Free Approach to Life & Food with 365-Day of Budget-Friendly & Easy-Breezy Air Fryer Recipes for Family and Friends

Albert K. Reich

Copyright© 2022 By Albert K. Reich All Rights Reserved

This book is copyright protected. It is only for personal use. You cannot amend, distribute, sell, use, quote or paraphrase any part of the content within this book, without the consent of the author or publisher.

Under no circumstances will any blame or legal responsibility be held against the publisher, or author, for any damages, reparation, or monetary loss due to the information contained within this book, either directly or indirectly.

Disclaimer Notice:

Please note the information contained within this document is for educational and entertainment purposes only. All effort has been executed to present accurate, up to date, reliable, complete information. No warranties of any kind are declared or implied. Readers acknowledge that the author is not engaged in the rendering of legal, financial, medical or professional advice. The content within this book has been derived from various sources. Please consult a licensed professional before attempting any techniques outlined in this book.

By reading this document, the reader agrees that under no circumstances is the author responsible for any losses, direct or indirect, that are incurred as a result of the use of the information contained within this document, including, but not limited to, errors, omissions, or inaccuracies.

Contents

Introduction 1

Chapter 1 Air Fryer Basic Guide 2

Chapter 2 Breakfasts 6

Chapter 3 Vegetables and Sides 11

Chapter 4 Poultry 16

Chapter 5 Fish and Seafood 22

Chapter 6 Beef, Pork, and Lamb 29

Chapter 7 Snacks and Appetisers 35

Chapter 8 Desserts 41

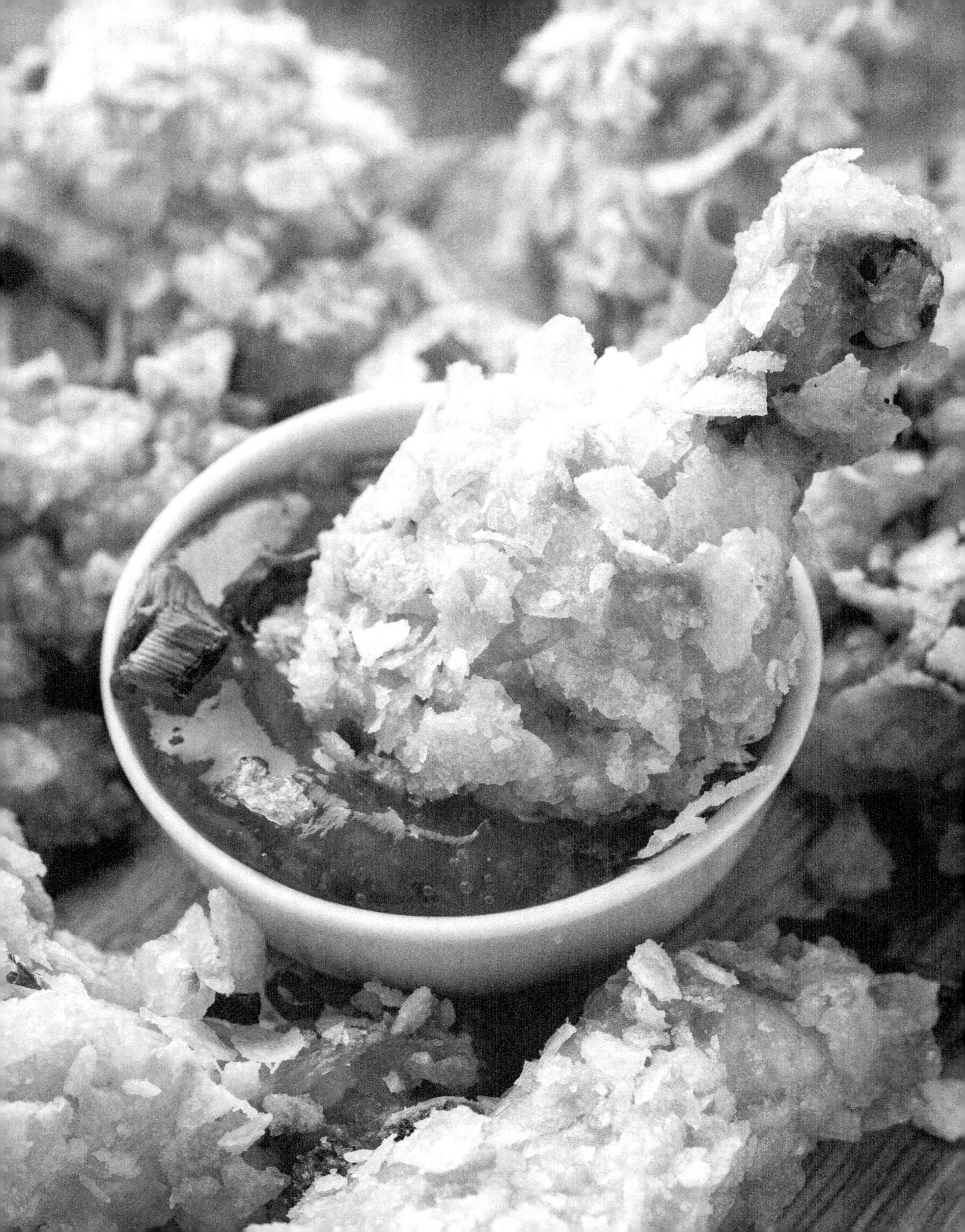

INTRODUCTION

The earliest models of air fryers introduced around 2010 immediately caught the attention of customers around the world. The advantages over conventional frying methods were plain to see. There was no danger from hot cooking oil boiling over, the food was quick to cook and best of all the food had a delicious fried texture and aroma but with a fraction of the calories.

By the following decade, the popularity of air fryers had grown to such a degree that sales eclipsed other popular kitchen gadgets such as slow cookers and blenders. Air fryer customers were using them regularly too. They were not some gadgets that were used only once and then pushed to the back of the cupboard. Tagine anyone?

For me, when I started using the air fryer, I was amazed at how easy it was to use this machine. I simply turned on the air fryer until it reached the right temperature, then I added the breaded chicken to the basket and pushed the drawer back in. Then in just a few minutes I had the most wonderfully crispy and juicy fried chicken without the usual greasiness.

Many cooks find it easiest to stand the air fryer on the kitchen counter and cook food in that position. Personally, I prefer to stand the air fryer on a thin wooden chopping board on top of the cooking rings of the stove. This means the air fryer has a stable base and any fumes from the machine can be extracted by the hood over the cooker. This almost eliminates cooking smells entering the living area.

The two most searched for air fryer recipes are air fryer chips and air fryer chicken. They're not the most imaginative of recipes, however, when you compare the cost of cooking chips in an air fryer (14.62p) to those cooked in a fan-assisted oven (35.38p), it is easy to understand why so many cooks turn to air fryers.

If you've never used an air fryer before, I think you will also be surprised at how easy it is to cook a wide range of recipes and how good the quality of the food that comes out is.

My cookbook covers breakfast dishes, vegetables, and sides, and then on includes main course dishes, such as poultry, beef, pork, lamb, fish, and seafood. Finally, there are two chapters on desserts, snacks, and appetisers.

So, what are some of the best things to cook in an air fryer? We've already mentioned that fried chicken and chips are everyone's favourite, but burgers, sausages and bacon all come out equally well too.

Even simple dishes such as leftovers can be quickly reheated in a bowl and given a deliciously crunchy crust. The only recipe that doesn't work in an air fryer is any food with a wet batter, for example, fried fish. So, this needs to be deep or shallow fried instead.

Some recipes in the cookbook are more involved than others, so if you're starting out, I would recommend trying the easiest ones first as you need to know and understand your air fryer.

Chapter 1 Air Fryer Basic Guide

As I started to use my air fryer more and more, I realised how versatile they can be. Initially, I thought about all the different fried foods that were so well suited to the way the cooker worked.

However, over time I discovered, that there are many more styles of cooking, such as roasting, grilling and baking, which give you just as good results. So, in addition to fried chicken, you can also try roasted or stuffed vegetables, corn on the cob, quick garlic bread and delicious scones.

One of my personal favourites is slices of banana, brushed with butter, and sprinkled with a little sugar. During cooking, the butter and sugar brown to give a delicious banana-flavoured caramel, which is great with a little vanilla ice cream.

How Do Air Fryers Work?

When I was getting some advice on the best model Tower air fryer to buy, I was given a quick comparison, which suddenly made it crystal clear to me how an air fryer works.

In fact, the air fryer is very similar to a convection oven, but the size of the cooking area is much smaller and the fan more powerful, so it circulates the very hot air all around the food to be cooked in the basket.

What's more, the ingredients are either gently tossed in a small amount of oil or sprayed using an aerosol. This thin coating of oil is still enough for the ingredient to brown and crisp but with a fraction of the calories of deep frying.

In addition, because the circulating air is generally at a higher temperature, the cooking and browning process is much quicker, saving electricity into the bargain.

Clearing up after cooking is no one's favourite task. However, I have developed my own technique. Often, if the basket and draw only contain a small amount of food residue, I find it easiest to add warm water and a little detergent and let it soak overnight. I then wash it in the sink the next day or put it through the dishwasher. It's very simple with minimum hassle.

Five Benefits of Using an Air Fryer

Less Fat

Test results show that air-fried food contains significantly less fat compared to food cooked in a convection oven or deep-fried - sometimes 70-80% less. With air frying, the food only needs a tiny amount of oil, like from an aerosol to start the complex browning reactions when the food is exposed to heat.

By using chunkier ingredients, for example, chunky chips instead of French fries, there is less surface area to coat with oil and consequently less oil use.

Quicker Cooking

My air fryer usually takes about four minutes to heat up to operating temperature, while my convection oven takes more than twice that. A further advantage in air fryers is that cooking times are significantly shorter than in convection ovens.

This is because the strong fan and compact shape of the air fryer allow the hot air to circulate around the food basket, transferring more heat directly to the ingredients and consequently cooking them quicker. As an example, chicken nuggets cooked in an air fryer take 15 minutes but up to 20-25 min in a convection oven.

Plenty of Recipes to Choose From

There are few recipes that you can't cook in an air fryer and usually, the ingredients that are best suited to air frying are the ones that need browning, such as burgers, pork chops, salmon fillets etc. Other similar ingredients include roasted vegetables, chips, brownies, cookies, and mini pizzas.

Less Energy

No one needs to be reminded about the soaring cost of domestic energy and so any kitchen device, which reduces costs, is going to be the first choice for most cooks. Cue the air fryer, with its compact cooking space and efficient fan, it can circulate hot air all around the ingredients in the basket, cooking and browning them quickly and efficiently.

So, what are the potential savings? I discovered some research which demonstrated that in a test, pieces of glazed cauliflower took 15 mins at 200 deg C to cook in the air fryer, which only cost 20p including 3 mins heating up time. When the same quantity of cauliflower was cooked in a convection oven, it took 11 minutes for the oven to heat up to 200 deg C and a further 30 minutes to cook the cauliflower, costing 42p. So, you can save more than 50% on electricity costs with an air fryer. A considerable saving in these days of runaway bills.

Enough Capacity

When I was deciding about which size air fryer to go for, there were two main constraints:

1.For a family of four, will the air fryer have enough capacity for four portions in one batch?

2.Is a larger, family-sized air fryer easy to lift and manoeuvre on the worktop?

A larger family air fryer with a capacity of 4 litres will be more than adequate to cook for larger portions at the same time. In addition, there will be enough space around the items being cooked to allow the hot air to circulate, producing even browning and cooking.

For manoeuvr ability, a family-size air fryer will weigh just over 4.5kg (10lbs), which for comparison is less than a tabletop stand food mixer. So, if there isn't enough space on the worktop for a permanent home for the air fryer, then it is straightforward to store it in a cupboard.

Air Fryer Cooking Tips

Preparing for Use

1.If you haven't used your air fryer before, follow the manufacturer's instructions for first-time use. This usually involves running the machine empty for a short period to eliminate any factory odours.

2.Always heat the air fryer up to the recipe temperature before adding the food to the basket. As with a conventional oven, this ensures the food heats up rapidly, lessening the chance of food poisoning.

3.For some foods which tend to stick, such as burgers and chicken thighs, it is worth oiling the grill of the basket with a pastry brush before use. Lightly brushing the food with oil as well to ensure that it doesn't stick during cooking. This makes the presentation better and cleaning the basket easier.

Air Frying

1.Don't be tempted to overfill the air fryer basket - think in terms of a single layer. The air fryer design requires that hot air is free to circulate around the food to cook it and brown it. If the basket is too full or the food too compacted, only the outer surfaces will cook, potentially leaving the inside raw.

2.Don't use too much oil - it's not necessary. The flavour and crunch of air fryer cooked food is down to the rapidly circulating hot air. Either use a pastry brush or an oil aerosol to coat your ingredients before cooking. This will be more than enough to brown and crisp the food. Using less oil also reduces cooking smells and of course, calories.

3.When cooking moist ingredients, such as roast vegetables, pat them dry with a cloth before brushing them with oil. If there is too much moisture in the air fryer, the vegetables will steam rather than roast, giving an inferior flavour.

Care and Cleaning

Keep your air fryer clean. Try to get into the habit of cleaning your air fryer after each time you use it. The basket may appear clean after a couple of uses, but you will find the smoke and odours produced during cooking increase.

Over time these may well end up tainting the flavour of the food you're cooking. If you get into the habit of cleaning your air fryer after each use, you will notice the improvement in the quality of the cooked food.

Cleaning is very simple. Half fill the basket with water and detergent, leave to soak, brush and rinse. Alternatively, if your manufacturer recommends it, clean it in the dishwasher.

Keep the exterior of your air fryer clean with a sponge and soapy water. Make sure the sponge is quite dry when you use it, as you don't want water getting into the electrics.

Air Fryer Q&A

1. Do I always need to brush ingredients with oil?

No. Only brush those ingredients you want to brown.

2. Do air fryers keep the nutrients in the food?

Yes. Because the cooking time is so much quicker, fewer vitamins and minerals will be destroyed.

3. Can you use trays and tins for cooking in the air fryer?

Yes. Some dishes have more liquid or have sauces, but they can still be cooked in a tray in the air fryer.

4. Can you open an air fryer while it's cooking?

Yes, but not for long. If you just want to check a dish isn't burning, a quick look won't do any harm. Releasing steam from the air fryer will brown the food quicker.

5. Can you reheat leftovers in an air fryer?

Yes. Air fryer leftovers are very popular because they brown and crisp during reheating making them more tasty.

6. Can you use silicon moulds in an air fryer?

Always check your manufacturer's recommendations but most silicon moulds are fine in an air fryer.

Chapter 2 Breakfasts

Bunless Breakfast Turkey Burgers

Prep time: 5 minutes | Cook time: 15 minutes | Serves 4

455 g ground turkey sausage, skinned
½ teaspoon salt
¼ teaspoon ground black pepper
30 g seeded and chopped green bell pepper
2 tablespoons mayonnaise
1 medium avocado, peeled, pitted, and sliced

1. In a large bowl, mix sausage with salt, black pepper, bell pepper, and mayonnaise. Form meat into four patties. 2. Place patties into ungreased air fryer basket. Adjust the temperature to 188°C and air fry for 15 minutes, turning patties halfway through cooking. Burgers will be done when dark brown and they have an internal temperature of at least 76°C. 3. Serve burgers topped with avocado slices on four medium plates.

Hole in One

Prep time: 5 minutes | Cook time: 6 to 7 minutes | Serves 1

1 slice bread
1 teaspoon soft butter
1 egg
Salt and pepper, to taste
1 tablespoon shredded Cheddar cheese
2 teaspoons diced ham

1. Place a baking dish inside air fryer basket and preheat the air fryer to 164°C. 2. Using a 2½-inch-diameter biscuit cutter, cut a hole in center of bread slice. 3. Spread softened butter on both sides of bread. 4. Lay bread slice in baking dish and crack egg into the hole. Sprinkle egg with salt and pepper to taste. 5. Cook for 5 minutes. 6. Turn toast over and top it with shredded cheese and diced ham. 7. Cook for 1 to 2 more minutes or until yolk is done to your liking.

Banana-Nut Muffins

Prep time: 5 minutes | Cook time: 15 minutes | Makes 10 muffins

Oil, for spraying
2 very ripe bananas
60 g packed light brown sugar
80 ml rapeseed oil or vegetable oil
1 large egg
1 teaspoon vanilla extract
95 g plain flour
1 teaspoon baking powder
1 teaspoon ground cinnamon
60 g chopped walnuts

1. Preheat the air fryer to 160°C. Spray 10 silicone muffin cups lightly with oil. 2. In a medium bowl, mash the bananas. Add the brown sugar, canola oil, egg, and vanilla and stir to combine. 3. Fold in the flour, baking powder, and cinnamon until just combined. 4. Add the walnuts and fold a few times to distribute throughout the batter. 5. Divide the batter equally among the prepared muffin cups and place them in the basket. You may need to work in batches, depending on the size of your air fryer. 6. Cook for 15 minutes, or until golden brown and a toothpick inserted into the center of a muffin comes out clean. The air fryer tends to brown muffins more than the oven, so don't be alarmed if they are darker than you're used to. They will still taste great. 7. Let cool on a wire rack before serving.

Spinach and Mushroom Mini Quiche

Prep time: 10 minutes | Cook time: 15 minutes | Serves 4

1 teaspoon olive oil, plus more for spraying
125 g coarsely chopped mushrooms
20 g fresh baby spinach, shredded
4 eggs, beaten
60 g shredded Cheddar cheese
60 g shredded Mozzarella cheese
¼ teaspoon salt
¼ teaspoon black pepper

1. Spray 4 silicone baking cups with olive oil and set aside. 2. In a medium sauté pan over medium heat, warm 1 teaspoon of olive oil. Add the mushrooms and sauté until soft, 3 to 4 minutes. 3. Add the spinach and cook until wilted, 1 to 2 minutes. Set aside. 4. In a medium bowl, whisk together the eggs, Cheddar cheese, Mozzarella cheese, salt, and pepper. 5. Gently fold the mushrooms and spinach into the egg mixture. 6. Pour ¼ of the mixture into each silicone baking cup. 7. Place the baking cups into the air fryer basket and air fry at 176°C for 5 minutes. Stir the mixture in each ramekin slightly and air fry until the egg has set, an additional 3 to 5 minutes.

Buffalo Chicken Breakfast Muffins

Prep time: 7 minutes | Cook time: 13 to 16 minutes | Serves 10

170 g shredded cooked chicken
85 g blue cheese, crumbled
2 tablespoons unsalted butter, melted
80 g Buffalo hot sauce, such as Frank's RedHot
1 teaspoon minced garlic
6 large eggs
Sea salt and freshly ground black pepper, to taste
Avocado oil spray

1. In a large bowl, stir together the chicken, blue cheese, melted butter, hot sauce, and garlic. 2. In a medium bowl or large liquid measuring cup, beat the eggs. Season with salt and pepper. 3. Spray 10 silicone muffin cups with oil. Divide the chicken mixture among the cups, and pour the egg mixture over top. 4. Place the cups in the air fryer and set to 148°C. Bake for 13 to 16 minutes, until the muffins are set and cooked through. (Depending on the size of your air fryer, you may need to cook the muffins in batches.)

BLT Breakfast Wrap

Prep time: 5 minutes | Cook time: 10 minutes | Serves 4

230 g reduced-sodium bacon
8 tablespoons mayonnaise
8 large romaine lettuce leaves
4 large plum tomatoes, sliced
Salt and freshly ground black pepper, to taste

1. Arrange the bacon in a single layer in the air fryer basket. (It's OK if the bacon sits a bit on the sides). Set the air fryer to 176ºC and air fry for 10 minutes. Check for crispiness and air fry for 2 to 3 minutes longer if needed. Cook in batches, if necessary, and drain the grease in between batches. 2. Spread 1 tablespoon of mayonnaise on each of the lettuce leaves and top with the tomatoes and cooked bacon. Season to taste with salt and freshly ground black pepper. Roll the lettuce leaves as you would a burrito, securing with a toothpick if desired.

Egg in a Hole

Prep time: 5 minutes | Cook time: 5 minutes | Serves 1

1 slice bread
1 teaspoon butter, softened
1 egg
Salt and pepper, to taste
1 tablespoon shredded Cheddar cheese
2 teaspoons diced ham

1. Preheat the air fryer to 164ºC. Place a baking dish in the air fryer basket. 2. On a flat work surface, cut a hole in the center of the bread slice with a 2½-inch-diameter biscuit cutter. 3. Spread the butter evenly on each side of the bread slice and transfer to the baking dish. 4. Crack the egg into the hole and season as desired with salt and pepper. Scatter the shredded cheese and diced ham on top. 5. Bake in the preheated air fryer for 5 minutes until the bread is lightly browned and the egg is cooked to your preference. 6. Remove from the basket and serve hot.

Steak and Eggs

Prep time: 8 minutes | Cook time: 14 minutes per batch | Serves 4

Cooking oil spray
4 (110 g) sirloin steaks
1 teaspoon granulated garlic, divided
1 teaspoon salt, divided
1 teaspoon freshly ground black pepper, divided
4 eggs
½ teaspoon paprika

1. Insert the crisper plate into the basket and the basket into the unit. Preheat the unit by selecting AIR FRY, setting the temperature to 184ºC, and setting the time to 3 minutes. Select START/STOP to begin. 2. Once the unit is preheated, spray the crisper plate with cooking oil. Place 2 steaks into the basket; do not oil or season them at this time. 3. Select AIR FRY, set the temperature to 184ºC, and set the time to 9 minutes. Select START/STOP to begin. 4. After 5 minutes, open the unit and flip the steaks. Sprinkle each with ¼ teaspoon of granulated garlic, ¼ teaspoon of salt, and ¼ teaspoon of pepper. Resume cooking until the steaks register at least 64ºC on a food thermometer. 5. When the cooking is complete, transfer the steaks to a plate and tent with aluminum foil to keep warm. Repeat steps 2, 3, and 4 with the remaining steaks. 6. Spray 4 ramekins with olive oil. Crack 1 egg into each ramekin. Sprinkle the eggs with the paprika and remaining ½ teaspoon each of salt and pepper. Working in batches, place 2 ramekins into the basket. 7. Select BAKE, set the temperature to 164ºC, and set the time to 5 minutes. Select START/STOP to begin. 8. When the cooking is complete and the eggs are cooked to 72ºC, remove the ramekins and repeat step 7 with the remaining 2 ramekins. 9. Serve the eggs with the steaks.

Everything Bagels

Prep time: 15 minutes | Cook time: 14 minutes | Makes 6 bagels

220 g shredded Mozzarella cheese or goat cheese Mozzarella
2 tablespoons unsalted butter or coconut oil
1 large egg, beaten
1 tablespoon apple cider vinegar
125 g blanched almond flour
1 tablespoon baking powder
⅛ teaspoon fine sea salt
1½ teaspoons everything bagel seasoning

1. Make the dough: Put the Mozzarella and butter in a large microwave-safe bowl and microwave for 1 to 2 minutes, until the cheese is entirely melted. Stir well. Add the egg and vinegar. Using a hand mixer on medium, combine well. Add the almond flour, baking powder, and salt and, using the mixer, combine well. 2. Lay a piece of baking paper on the countertop and place the dough on it. Knead it for about 3 minutes. The dough should be a little sticky but pliable. (If the dough is too sticky, chill it in the refrigerator for an hour or overnight.) 3. Preheat the air fryer to 176ºC. Spray a baking sheet or pie pan that will fit into your air fryer with avocado oil. 4. Divide the dough into 6 equal portions. Roll 1 portion into a log that is 6 inches long and about ½ inch thick. Form the log into a circle and seal the edges together, making a bagel shape. Repeat with the remaining portions of dough, making 6 bagels. 5. Place the bagels on the greased baking sheet. Spray the bagels with avocado oil and top with everything bagel seasoning, pressing the seasoning into the dough with your hands. 6. Place the bagels in the air fryer and bake for 14 minutes, or until cooked through and golden brown, flipping after 6 minutes. 7. Remove the bagels from the air fryer and allow them to cool slightly before slicing them in half and serving. Store leftovers in an airtight container in the fridge for up to 4 days or in the freezer for up to a month.

Jalapeño Popper Egg Cups

Prep time: 10 minutes | Cook time: 10 minutes | Serves 2

4 large eggs
30 g chopped pickled jalapeños
60 g full-fat cream cheese
60 g shredded sharp Cheddar cheese

1. In a medium bowl, beat the eggs, then pour into four silicone muffin cups. 2. In a large microwave-safe bowl, place jalapeños, cream cheese, and Cheddar. Microwave for 30 seconds and stir. Take a spoonful, approximately ¼ of the mixture, and place it in the center of one of the egg cups. Repeat with remaining mixture. 3. Place egg cups into the air fryer basket. 4. Adjust the temperature to 160ºC and bake for 10 minutes. 5. Serve warm.

Butternut Squash and Ricotta Frittata

Prep time: 10 minutes | Cook time: 33 minutes | Serves 2 to 3

160 g cubed (½-inch) butternut squash
2 tablespoons olive oil
Kosher or coarse sea salt and freshly ground black pepper, to taste
4 fresh sage leaves, thinly sliced
6 large eggs, lightly beaten
60 g ricotta cheese
Cayenne pepper

1. In a bowl, toss the squash with the olive oil and season with salt and black pepper until evenly coated. Sprinkle the sage on the bottom of a cake pan and place the squash on top. Place the pan in the air fryer and bake at 204ºC for 10 minutes. Stir to incorporate the sage, then cook until the squash is tender and lightly caramelised at the edges, about 3 minutes more. 2. Pour the eggs over the squash, dollop the ricotta all over, and sprinkle with cayenne. Bake at 148ºC until the eggs are set and the frittata is golden brown on top, about 20 minutes. Remove the pan from the air fryer and cut the frittata into wedges to serve.

Italian Egg Cups

Prep time: 5 minutes | Cook time: 10 minutes | Serves 4

Olive oil
240 ml ready-made marinara sauce
4 eggs
4 tablespoons shredded Mozzarella cheese
4 teaspoons grated Parmesan cheese
Salt and freshly ground black pepper, to taste
Chopped fresh basil, for garnish

1. Lightly spray 4 individual ramekins with olive oil. 2. Pour 60 ml marinara sauce into each ramekin. 3. Crack one egg into each ramekin on top of the marinara sauce. 4. Sprinkle 1 tablespoon of Mozzarella and 1 tablespoon of Parmesan on top of each egg. Season with salt and pepper. 5. Cover each ramekin with aluminum foil. Place two of the ramekins in the air fryer basket. 6. Air fry at 176ºC for 5 minutes and remove the aluminum foil. Air fry until the top is lightly browned and the egg white is cooked, another 2 to 4 minutes. If you prefer the yolk to be firmer, cook for 3 to 5 more minutes. 7. Repeat with the remaining two ramekins. Garnish with basil and serve.

Egg and Bacon Muffins

Prep time: 5 minutes | Cook time: 15 minutes | Serves 1

2 eggs
Salt and ground black pepper, to taste
1 tablespoon green pesto
85 g shredded Cheddar cheese
140 g cooked bacon
1 spring onion, chopped

1. Preheat the air fryer to 176ºC. Line a cupcake tin with baking paper. 2. Beat the eggs with pepper, salt, and pesto in a bowl. Mix in the cheese. 3. Pour the eggs into the cupcake tin and top with the bacon and spring onion. 4. Bake in the preheated air fryer for 15 minutes, or until the egg is set. 5. Serve immediately.

Breakfast Meatballs

Prep time: 10 minutes | Cook time: 15 minutes | Makes 18 meatballs

455 g ground herbed pork sausage meat
½ teaspoon salt
¼ teaspoon ground black pepper
60 g shredded sharp Cheddar cheese
30 g cream cheese, softened
1 large egg, whisked

1. Combine all ingredients in a large bowl. Form mixture into eighteen 1-inch meatballs. 2. Place meatballs into ungreased air fryer basket. Adjust the temperature to 204ºC and air fry for 15 minutes, shaking basket three times during cooking. Meatballs will be browned on the outside and have an internal temperature of at least 64ºC when completely cooked. Serve warm.

Pancake Cake

Prep time: 10 minutes | Cook time: 7 minutes | Serves 4

60 g blanched finely ground almond flour
30 g powdered sweetener
½ teaspoon baking powder
2 tablespoons unsalted butter, softened
1 large egg
½ teaspoon unflavored gelatin
½ teaspoon vanilla extract
½ teaspoon ground cinnamon

1. In a large bowl, mix almond flour, sweetener, and baking powder. Add butter, egg, gelatin, vanilla, and cinnamon. Pour into a round baking pan. 2. Place pan into the air fryer basket. 3. Adjust the temperature to 148ºC and set the timer for 7 minutes. 4. When the cake is completely cooked, a toothpick will come out clean. Cut cake into four and serve.

Mozzarella Bacon Calzones

Prep time: 15 minutes | Cook time: 12 minutes | Serves 4

2 large eggs
125 g blanched finely ground almond flour
250 g shredded Mozzarella cheese
60 g cream cheese, softened and broken into small pieces
4 slices cooked bacon, crumbled

1. Beat eggs in a small bowl. Pour into a medium nonstick skillet over medium heat and scramble. Set aside. 2. In a large microwave-safe bowl, mix flour and MozzarellAdd cream cheese to the bowl. 3. Place bowl in microwave and cook 45 seconds on high to melt cheese, then stir with a fork until a soft dough ball forms. 4. Cut a piece of baking paper to fit air fryer basket. Separate dough into two sections and press each out into an 8-inch round. 5. On half of each dough round, place half of the scrambled eggs and crumbled bacon. Fold the other side of the dough over and press to seal the edges. 6. Place calzones on ungreased baking paper and into air fryer basket. Adjust the temperature to 176ºC and set the timer for 12 minutes, turning calzones halfway through cooking. Crust will be golden and firm when done. 7. Let calzones cool on a cooking rack 5 minutes before serving.

Broccoli-Mushroom Frittata

Prep time: 10 minutes | Cook time: 20 minutes | Serves 2

1 tablespoon olive oil	½ teaspoon salt
185 g broccoli florets, finely chopped	¼ teaspoon freshly ground black pepper
60 g sliced brown mushrooms	6 eggs
30 g finely chopped onion	30 g Parmesan cheese

1. In a nonstick cake pan, combine the olive oil, broccoli, mushrooms, onion, salt, and pepper. Stir until the vegetables are thoroughly coated with oil. Place the cake pan in the air fryer basket and set the air fryer to 204°C. Air fry for 5 minutes until the vegetables soften. 2. Meanwhile, in a medium bowl, whisk the eggs and Parmesan until thoroughly combined. Pour the egg mixture into the pan and shake gently to distribute the vegetables. Air fry for another 15 minutes until the eggs are set. 3. Remove from the air fryer and let sit for 5 minutes to cool slightly. Use a silicone spatula to gently lift the frittata onto a plate before serving.

Bacon Muffin Sandwiches

Prep time: 5 minutes | Cook time: 8 minutes | Serves 4

4 English muffins, split	4 slices cheese
8 bacon medallions	Cooking spray

1. Preheat the air fryer to 188°C. 2. Make the sandwiches: Top each of 4 muffin halves with 2 slices of Canadian bacon, 1 slice of cheese, and finish with the remaining muffin half. 3. Put the sandwiches in the air fryer basket and spritz the tops with cooking spray. 4. Bake for 4 minutes. Flip the sandwiches and bake for another 4 minutes. 5. Divide the sandwiches among four plates and serve warm.

Breakfast Calzone

Prep time: 15 minutes | Cook time: 15 minutes | Serves 4

185 g shredded Mozzarella cheese	4 large eggs, scrambled
60 g blanched finely ground almond flour	230 g cooked sausage meat, crumbled
30 g full-fat cream cheese	8 tablespoons shredded mild Cheddar cheese
1 large whole egg	

1. In a large microwave-safe bowl, add Mozzarella, almond flour, and cream cheese. Microwave for 1 minute. Stir until the mixture is smooth and forms a ball. Add the egg and stir until dough forms. 2. Place dough between two sheets of baking paper and roll out to ¼-inch thickness. Cut the dough into four rectangles. 3. Mix scrambled eggs and cooked sausage together in a large bowl. Divide the mixture evenly among each piece of dough, placing it on the lower half of the rectangle. Sprinkle each with 2 tablespoons Cheddar. 4. Fold over the rectangle to cover the egg and meat mixture. Pinch, roll, or use a wet fork to close the edges completely. 5. Cut a piece of baking paper to fit your air fryer basket and place the calzones onto the baking paper. Place baking paper into the air fryer basket. 6. Adjust the temperature to 192°C and air fry for 15 minutes. 7. Flip the calzones halfway through the cooking time. When done, calzones should be golden in color. Serve immediately.

Sausage and Egg Breakfast Burrito

Prep time: 5 minutes | Cook time: 30 minutes | Serves 6

6 eggs	230 g ground chicken sausage
Salt and pepper, to taste	125 g salsa
Cooking oil	6 medium (8-inch) flour tortillas
60 g chopped red bell pepper	60 g shredded Cheddar cheese
60 g chopped green bell pepper	

1. In a medium bowl, whisk the eggs. Add salt and pepper to taste. 2. Place a skillet on medium-high heat. Spray with cooking oil. Add the eggs. Scramble for 2 to 3 minutes, until the eggs are fluffy. Remove the eggs from the skillet and set aside. 3. If needed, spray the skillet with more oil. Add the chopped red and green bell peppers. Cook for 2 to 3 minutes, until the peppers are soft. 4. Add the ground sausage to the skillet. Break the sausage into smaller pieces using a spatula or spoon. Cook for 3 to 4 minutes, until the sausage is brown. 5. Add the salsa and scrambled eggs. Stir to combine. Remove the skillet from heat. 6. Spoon the mixture evenly onto the tortillas. 7. To form the burritos, fold the sides of each tortilla in toward the middle and then roll up from the bottom. You can secure each burrito with a toothpick. Or you can moisten the outside edge of the tortilla with a small amount of water. I prefer to use a cooking brush, but you can also dab with your fingers. 8. Spray the burritos with cooking oil and place them in the air fryer. Do not stack. Cook the burritos in batches if they do not all fit in the basket. Air fry at 204°C for 8 minutes. 9. Open the air fryer and flip the burritos. Cook for an additional 2 minutes or until crisp. 10. If necessary, repeat steps 8 and 9 for the remaining burritos. 11. Sprinkle the Cheddar cheese over the burritos. Cool before serving.

Drop Biscuits

Prep time: 10 minutes | Cook time: 9 to 10 minutes | Serves 5

500 g plain flour	for brushing on the biscuits (optional)
1 tablespoon baking powder	
1 tablespoon sugar (optional)	185 ml buttermilk
1 teaspoon salt	1 to 2 tablespoons oil
6 tablespoons butter, plus more	

1. In a large bowl, whisk the flour, baking powder, sugar (if using), and salt until blended. 2. Add the butter. Using a pastry cutter or 2 forks, work the dough until pea-sized balls of the butter-flour mixture appear. Stir in the buttermilk until the mixture is sticky. 3. Preheat the air fryer to 164°C. Line the air fryer basket with baking paper and spritz it with oil. 4. Drop the dough by the tablespoonful onto the prepared basket, leaving 1 inch between each, to form 10 biscuits. 5. Bake for 5 minutes. Flip the biscuits and cook for 4 minutes more for a light brown top, or 5 minutes more for a darker biscuit. Brush the tops with melted butter, if desired.

Creamy Cinnamon Rolls

Prep time: 10 minutes | Cook time: 9 minutes | Serves 8

455 g frozen shortcrust pastry, thawed
60 g butter, melted
95 g brown sugar
1½ tablespoons ground cinnamon
Cream Cheese Glaze:
110 g cream cheese, softened
2 tablespoons butter, softened
160 g powdered sugar
½ teaspoon vanilla extract

1. Let the bread dough come to room temperature on the counter. On a lightly floured surface, roll the dough into a 13-inch by 11-inch rectangle. Position the rectangle so the 13-inch side is facing you. Brush the melted butter all over the dough, leaving a 1-inch border uncovered along the edge farthest away from you. 2. Combine the brown sugar and cinnamon in a small bowl. Sprinkle the mixture evenly over the buttered dough, keeping the 1-inch border uncovered. Roll the dough into a log, starting with the edge closest to you. Roll the dough tightly, rolling evenly, and push out any air pockets. When you get to the uncovered edge of the dough, press the dough onto the roll to seal it together. 3. Cut the log into 8 pieces, slicing slowly with a sawing motion so you don't flatten the dough. Turn the slices on their sides and cover with a clean kitchen towel. Let the rolls sit in the warmest part of the kitchen for 1½ to 2 hours to rise. 4. To make the glaze, place the cream cheese and butter in a microwave-safe bowl. Soften the mixture in the microwave for 30 seconds at a time until it is easy to stir. Gradually add the powdered sugar and stir to combine. Add the vanilla extract and whisk until smooth. Set aside. 5. When the rolls have risen, preheat the air fryer to 176°C. 6. Transfer 4 of the rolls to the air fryer basket. Air fry for 5 minutes. Turn the rolls over and air fry for another 4 minutes. Repeat with the remaining 4 rolls. 7. Let the rolls cool for two minutes before glazing. Spread large dollops of cream cheese glaze on top of the warm cinnamon rolls, allowing some glaze to drip down the side of the rolls. Serve warm.

Asparagus and Bell Pepper Strata

Prep time: 10 minutes | Cook time: 14 to 20 minutes | Serves 4

8 large asparagus spears, trimmed and cut into 2-inch pieces
40 g shredded carrot
60 g chopped red bell pepper
2 slices low-sodium whole-wheat bread, cut into ½-inch cubes
3 egg whites
1 egg
3 tablespoons skimmed milk
½ teaspoon dried thyme

1. In a baking pan, combine the asparagus, carrot, red bell pepper, and 1 tablespoon of water. Bake in the air fryer at 164°C for 3 to 5 minutes, or until crisp-tender. Drain well. 2. Add the bread cubes to the vegetables and gently toss. 3. In a medium bowl, whisk the egg whites, egg, milk, and thyme until frothy. 4. Pour the egg mixture into the pan. Bake for 11 to 15 minutes, or until the strata is slightly puffy and set and the top starts to brown. Serve.

Chapter 3 Vegetables and Sides

Citrus-Roasted Broccoli Florets

Prep time: 5 minutes | Cook time: 12 minutes | Serves 6

500 g broccoli florets (approximately 1 large head)
2 tablespoons olive oil
½ teaspoon salt
125 ml orange juice
1 tablespoon raw honey
Orange wedges, for serving (optional)

1. Preheat the air fryer to 184°C. 2. In a large bowl, combine the broccoli, olive oil, salt, orange juice, and honey. Toss the broccoli in the liquid until well coated. 3. Pour the broccoli mixture into the air fryer basket and roast for 6 minutes. Stir and roast for 6 minutes more. 4. Serve alone or with orange wedges for additional citrus flavor, if desired.

Parmesan-Rosemary Radishes

Prep time: 5 minutes | Cook time: 15 to 20 minutes | Serves 4

1 bunch radishes, stemmed, trimmed, and quartered
1 tablespoon avocado oil
2 tablespoons finely grated fresh Parmesan cheese
1 tablespoon chopped fresh rosemary
Sea salt and freshly ground black pepper, to taste

1. Place the radishes in a medium bowl and toss them with the avocado oil, Parmesan cheese, rosemary, salt, and pepper. 2. Set the air fryer to 192°C. Arrange the radishes in a single layer in the air fryer basket. Roast for 15 to 20 minutes, until golden brown and tender. Let cool for 5 minutes before serving.

Radish Chips

Prep time: 10 minutes | Cook time: 5 minutes | Serves 4

500 ml water
455 g radishes
¼ teaspoon onion powder
¼ teaspoon paprika
½ teaspoon garlic powder
2 tablespoons coconut oil, melted

1. Place water in a medium saucepan and bring to a boil on stovetop. 2. Remove the top and bottom from each radish, then use a mandoline to slice each radish thin and uniformly. You may also use the slicing blade in the food processor for this step. 3. Place the radish slices into the boiling water for 5 minutes or until translucent. Remove them from the water and place them into a clean kitchen towel to absorb excess moisture. 4. Toss the radish chips in a large bowl with remaining ingredients until fully coated in oil and seasoning. Place radish chips into the air fryer basket. 5. Adjust the temperature to 160°C and air fry for 5 minutes. 6. Shake the basket two or three times during the cooking time. Serve warm.

Broccoli-Cheddar Twice-Baked Potatoes

Prep time: 10 minutes | Cook time: 46 minutes | Serves 4

Oil, for spraying
2 medium russet potatoes
1 tablespoon olive oil
30 g broccoli florets
1 tablespoon sour cream
1 teaspoon garlic granules
1 teaspoon onion powder
60 g shredded Cheddar cheese

1. Line the air fryer basket with baking paper and spray lightly with oil. 2. Rinse the potatoes and pat dry with paper towels. Rub the outside of the potatoes with the olive oil and place them in the prepared basket. 3. Air fry at 204°C for 40 minutes, or until easily pierced with a fork. Let cool just enough to handle, then cut the potatoes in half lengthwise. 4. Meanwhile, place the broccoli in a microwave-safe bowl, cover with water, and microwave on high for 5 to 8 minutes. Drain and set aside. 5. Scoop out most of the potato flesh and transfer to a medium bowl. 6. Add the sour cream, garlic, and onion powder and stir until the potatoes are mashed. 7. Spoon the potato mixture back into the hollowed potato skins, mounding it to fit, if necessary. Top with the broccoli and cheese. Return the potatoes to the basket. You may need to work in batches, depending on the size of your air fryer. 8. Air fry at 204°C for 3 to 6 minutes, or until the cheese has melted. Serve immediately.

Roasted Sweet Potatoes

Prep time: 10 minutes | Cook time: 25 minutes | Serves 4

Cooking oil spray
2 sweet potatoes, peeled and cut into 1-inch cubes
1 tablespoon extra-virgin olive oil
Pinch salt
Freshly ground black pepper, to taste
½ teaspoon dried thyme
½ teaspoon dried marjoram
30 g grated Parmesan cheese

1. Insert the crisper plate into the basket and the basket into the unit. Preheat the unit by selecting AIR ROAST, setting the temperature to 164°C, and setting the time to 3 minutes. Select START/STOP to begin. 2. Once the unit is preheated, spray the crisper plate with cooking oil. Put the sweet potato cubes into the basket and drizzle with olive oil. Toss gently to coat. Sprinkle with the salt, pepper, thyme, and marjoram and toss again. 3. Select AIR ROAST, set the temperature to 164°C, and set the time to 25 minutes. Select START/STOP to begin. 4. After 10 minutes, remove the basket and shake the potatoes. Reinsert the basket to resume cooking. After another 10 minutes, remove the basket and shake the potatoes one more time. Sprinkle evenly with the Parmesan cheese. Reinsert the basket to resume cooking. 5. When the cooking is complete, the potatoes should be tender. Serve immediately.

Parsnip Fries with Romesco Sauce

Prep time: 20 minutes | Cook time: 24 minutes | Serves 4

Romesco Sauce:
1 red bell pepper, halved and seeded
1 (1-inch) thick slice of Italian bread, torn into pieces
125 g almonds, toasted
Olive oil
½ Jalapeño pepper, seeded
1 tablespoon fresh parsley leaves
1 clove garlic
2 plum tomatoes, peeled and seeded (or 40 g canned crushed tomatoes)
1 tablespoon red wine vinegar
¼ teaspoon smoked paprika
½ teaspoon salt
185 ml olive oil
3 parsnips, peeled and cut into long strips
2 teaspoons olive oil
Salt and freshly ground black pepper, to taste

1. Preheat the air fryer to 204ºC. 2. Place the red pepper halves, cut side down, in the air fryer basket and air fry for 8 to 10 minutes, or until the skin turns black all over. Remove the pepper from the air fryer and let it cool. When it is cool enough to handle, peel the pepper. 3. Toss the torn bread and almonds with a little olive oil and air fry for 4 minutes, shaking the basket a couple times throughout the cooking time. When the bread and almonds are nicely toasted, remove them from the air fryer and let them cool for just a minute or two. 4. Combine the toasted bread, almonds, roasted red pepper, Jalapeño pepper, parsley, garlic, tomatoes, vinegar, smoked paprika and salt in a food processor or blender. Process until smooth. With the processor running, add the olive oil through the feed tube until the sauce comes together in a smooth paste that is barely pourable. 5. Toss the parsnip strips with the olive oil, salt and freshly ground black pepper and air fry at 204ºC for 10 minutes, shaking the basket a couple times during the cooking process so they brown and cook evenly. Serve the parsnip fries warm with the Romesco sauce to dip into.

Garlic-Parmesan Crispy Baby Potatoes

Prep time: 10 minutes | Cook time: 15 minutes | Serves 4

Oil, for spraying
455 g baby potatoes
60 g grated Parmesan cheese, divided
3 tablespoons olive oil
2 teaspoons garlic granules
½ teaspoon onion powder
½ teaspoon salt
¼ teaspoon freshly ground black pepper
¼ teaspoon paprika
2 tablespoons chopped fresh parsley, for garnish

1. Line the air fryer basket with baking paper and spray lightly with oil. 2. Rinse the potatoes, pat dry with paper towels, and place in a large bowl. 3. In a small bowl, mix together 30 g Parmesan cheese, the olive oil, garlic, onion powder, salt, black pepper, and paprikPour the mixture over the potatoes and toss to coat. 4. Transfer the potatoes to the prepared basket and spread them out in an even layer, taking care to keep them from touching. You may need to work in batches, depending on the size of your air fryer. 5. Air fry at 204ºC for 15 minutes, stirring after 7 to 8 minutes, or until easily pierced with a fork. Continue to cook for another 1 to 2 minutes, if needed. 6. Sprinkle with the parsley and the remaining Parmesan cheese and serve.

Ratatouille

Prep time: 15 minutes | Cook time: 20 minutes | Serves 2 to 3

250 g ¾-inch cubed peeled aubergine
1 small red, yellow, or orange bell pepper, stemmed, seeded, and diced
125 g cherry tomatoes
6 to 8 cloves garlic, peeled and halved lengthwise
3 tablespoons olive oil
1 teaspoon dried oregano
½ teaspoon dried thyme
1 teaspoon kosher salt
½ teaspoon black pepper

1. In a medium bowl, combine the aubergine, bell pepper, tomatoes, garlic, oil, oregano, thyme, salt, and pepper. Toss to combine. 2. Place the vegetables in the air fryer basket. Set the air fryer to 204ºC for 20 minutes, or until the vegetables are crisp-tender.

Parmesan-Thyme Butternut Squash

Prep time: 15 minutes | Cook time: 20 minutes | Serves 4

310 g butternut squash, cubed into 1-inch pieces (approximately 1 medium)
2 tablespoons olive oil
¼ teaspoon salt
¼ teaspoon garlic powder
¼ teaspoon black pepper
1 tablespoon fresh thyme
30 g grated Parmesan

1. Preheat the air fryer to 184ºC. 2. In a large bowl, combine the cubed squash with the olive oil, salt, garlic powder, pepper, and thyme until the squash is well coated. 3. Pour this mixture into the air fryer basket, and roast for 10 minutes. Stir and roast another 8 to 10 minutes more. 4. Remove the squash from the air fryer and toss with freshly grated Parmesan before serving.

Mashed Sweet Potato Tots

Prep time: 10 minutes | Cook time: 12 to 13 minutes per batch | Makes 18 to 24 tots

125 g cooked mashed sweet potatoes
1 egg white, beaten
⅛ teaspoon ground cinnamon
1 dash nutmeg
2 tablespoons chopped pecans
1½ teaspoons honey
Salt, to taste
60 g panko bread crumbs
Oil for misting or cooking spray

1. Preheat the air fryer to 200ºC. 2. In a large bowl, mix together the potatoes, egg white, cinnamon, nutmeg, pecans, honey, and salt to taste. 3. Place panko crumbs on a sheet of wax paper. 4. For each tot, use about 2 teaspoons of sweet potato mixture. To shape, drop the measure of potato mixture onto panko crumbs and push crumbs up and around potatoes to coat edges. Then turn tot over to coat other side with crumbs. 5. Mist tots with oil or cooking spray and place in air fryer basket in single layer. 6. Air fry at 200ºC for 12 to 13 minutes, until browned and crispy. 7. Repeat steps 5 and 6 to cook remaining tots.

Parmesan and Herb Sweet Potatoes

Prep time: 10 minutes | Cook time: 18 minutes | Serves 4

2 large sweet potatoes, peeled and cubed
65 ml olive oil
1 teaspoon dried rosemary
½ teaspoon salt
2 tablespoons shredded Parmesan

1. Preheat the air fryer to 184°C. 2. In a large bowl, toss the sweet potatoes with the olive oil, rosemary, and salt. 3. Pour the potatoes into the air fryer basket and roast for 10 minutes, then stir the potatoes and sprinkle the Parmesan over the top. Continue roasting for 8 minutes more. 4. Serve hot and enjoy.

Chermoula-Roasted Beets

Prep time: 15 minutes | Cook time: 25 minutes | Serves 4

Chermoula:
20 g packed fresh coriander leaves
10 g packed fresh parsley leaves
6 cloves garlic, peeled
2 teaspoons smoked paprika
2 teaspoons ground cumin
1 teaspoon ground coriander
½ to 1 teaspoon cayenne pepper
Pinch crushed saffron (optional)
125 ml extra-virgin olive oil
Kosher or coarse sea salt, to taste
Beets:
3 medium beetroot, trimmed, peeled, and cut into 1-inch chunks
2 tablespoons chopped fresh coriander
2 tablespoons chopped fresh parsley

1. For the chermoula: In a food processor, combine the coriander leaves, parsley, garlic, paprika, cumin, coriander, and cayenne. Pulse until coarsely chopped. Add the saffron, if using, and process until combined. With the food processor running, slowly add the olive oil in a steady stream; process until the sauce is uniform. Season to taste with salt. 2. For the beets: In a large bowl, drizzle the beetroot with 125 g the chermoula, or enough to coat. Arrange the beetroot in the air fryer basket. Set the air fryer to 192°C for 25 to minutes, or until the beetroot is tender. 3. Transfer the beetroot to a serving platter. Sprinkle with chopped coriander and parsley and serve.

Roasted Potatoes and Asparagus

Prep time: 5 minutes | Cook time: 23 minutes | Serves 4

4 medium potatoes
1 bunch asparagus
40 g cottage cheese
80 g low-fat crème fraiche
1 tablespoon wholegrain mustard
Salt and pepper, to taste
Cooking spray

1. Preheat the air fryer to 200°C. Spritz the air fryer basket with cooking spray. 2. Place the potatoes in the basket. Air fry the potatoes for 20 minutes. 3. Boil the asparagus in salted water for 3 minutes. 4. Remove the potatoes and mash them with rest of ingredients. Sprinkle with salt and pepper. 5. Serve immediately.

Hawaiian Brown Rice

Prep time: 10 minutes | Cook time: 12 to 16 minutes | Serves 4 to 6

110 g minced pork
1 teaspoon butter
30 g minced onion
30 g minced bell pepper
250 g cooked brown rice
1 (230 g) can crushed pineapple, drained

1. Shape pork mince into 3 or 4 thin patties. Air fry at 200°C for 6 to 8 minutes or until well done. Remove from air fryer, drain, and crumble. Set aside. 2. Place butter, onion, and bell pepper in baking pan. Roast at 200°C for 1 minute and stir. Cook 3 to 4 minutes longer or just until vegetables are tender. 3. Add pork mince, rice, and pineapple to vegetables and stir together. 4. Roast for 2 to 3 minutes, until heated through.

Stuffed Red Peppers with Herbed Ricotta and Tomatoes

Prep time: 10 minutes | Cook time: 20 minutes | Serves 4

2 red bell peppers
125 g cooked brown rice
2 plum tomatoes, diced
1 garlic clove, minced
¼ teaspoon salt
¼ teaspoon black pepper
110 g ricotta
3 tablespoons fresh basil, chopped
3 tablespoons fresh oregano, chopped
30 g shredded Parmesan, for topping

1. Preheat the air fryer to 184°C. 2. Cut the bell peppers in half and remove the seeds and stem. 3. In a medium bowl, combine the brown rice, tomatoes, garlic, salt, and pepper. 4. Distribute the rice filling evenly among the four bell pepper halves. 5. In a small bowl, combine the ricotta, basil, and oregano. Put the herbed cheese over the top of the rice mixture in each bell pepper. 6. Place the bell peppers into the air fryer and roast for 20 minutes. 7. Remove and serve with shredded Parmesan on top.

Sesame ginger Broccoli

Prep time: 10 minutes | Cook time: 15 minutes | Serves 4

3 tablespoons toasted sesame oil
2 teaspoons sesame seeds
1 tablespoon chilli garlic sauce
2 teaspoons minced fresh ginger
½ teaspoon kosher or coarse sea salt
½ teaspoon black pepper
1 (455 g) frozen broccoli florets (do not thaw)

1. In a large bowl, combine the sesame oil, sesame seeds, chilli garlic sauce, ginger, salt, and pepper. Stir until well combined. Add the broccoli and toss until well coated. 2. Arrange the broccoli in the air fryer basket. Set the air fryer to 164°C for 15 minutes, or until the broccoli is crisp, tender, and the edges are lightly browned, gently tossing halfway through the cooking time.

Crispy Courgette Sticks

Prep time: 5 minutes | Cook time: 14 minutes | Serves 4

2 small courgettes, cut into 2-inch × ½-inch sticks
3 tablespoons chickpea flour
2 teaspoons arrowroot (or cornflour)
½ teaspoon garlic granules
¼ teaspoon sea salt
⅛ teaspoon freshly ground black pepper
1 tablespoon water
Cooking spray

1. Preheat the air fryer to 200ºC. 2. Combine the courgette sticks with the chickpea flour, arrowroot, garlic granules, salt, and pepper in a medium bowl and toss to coat. Add the water and stir to mix well. 3. Spritz the air fryer basket with cooking spray and spread out the courgette sticks in the basket. Mist the courgette sticks with cooking spray. 4. Air fry for 14 minutes, shaking the basket halfway through, or until the courgette sticks are crispy and nicely browned. 5. Serve warm.

Blistered Shishito Peppers with Lime Juice

Prep time: 5 minutes | Cook time: 9 minutes | Serves 3

230 g Shishito peppers, rinsed
Cooking spray
Sauce:
1 tablespoon tamari or shoyu
2 teaspoons fresh lime juice
2 large garlic cloves, minced

1. Preheat the air fryer to 200ºC. Spritz the air fryer basket with cooking spray. 2. Place the Shishito peppers in the basket and spritz them with cooking spray. Roast for 3 minutes. 3. Meanwhile, whisk together all the ingredients for the sauce in a large bowl. Set aside. 4. Shake the basket and spritz them with cooking spray again, then roast for an additional 3 minutes. 5. Shake the basket one more time and spray the peppers with cooking spray. Continue roasting for 3 minutes until the peppers are blistered and nicely browned. 6. Remove the peppers from the basket to the bowl of sauce. Toss to coat well and serve immediately.

Garlic Roasted Broccoli

Prep time: 8 minutes | Cook time: 10 to 14 minutes | Serves 6

1 head broccoli, cut into bite-sized florets
1 tablespoon avocado oil
2 teaspoons minced garlic
⅛ teaspoon red pepper flakes
Sea salt and freshly ground black pepper, to taste
1 tablespoon freshly squeezed lemon juice
½ teaspoon lemon zest

1. In a large bowl, toss together the broccoli, avocado oil, garlic, red pepper flakes, salt, and pepper. 2. Set the air fryer to 192ºC. Arrange the broccoli in a single layer in the air fryer basket, working in batches if necessary. Roast for 10 to 14 minutes, until the broccoli is lightly charred. 3. Place the florets in a medium bowl and toss with the lemon juice and lemon zest. Serve.

Marinara Pepperoni Mushroom Pizza

Prep time: 5 minutes | Cook time: 18 minutes | Serves 4

4 large Portobello mushrooms, stems removed
4 teaspoons olive oil
240 g ready-made marinara sauce
125 g shredded Mozzarella cheese
10 slices sugar-free pepperoni

1. Preheat the air fryer to 192ºC. 2. Brush each mushroom cap with the olive oil, one teaspoon for each cap. 3. Put on a baking sheet and bake, stem-side down, for 8 minutes. 4. Take out of the air fryer and divide the marinara sauce, Mozzarella cheese and pepperoni evenly among the caps. 5. Air fry for another 10 minutes until browned. 6. Serve hot.

Asian-Inspired Roasted Broccoli

Prep time: 10 minutes | Cook time: 15 minutes | Serves 4

Broccoli:
Oil, for spraying
455 g broccoli florets
2 teaspoons peanut oil
1 tablespoon minced garlic
½ teaspoon salt
Sauce:
2 tablespoons soy sauce
2 teaspoons honey
2 teaspoons Sriracha
1 teaspoon rice vinegar

Make the Broccoli: 1. Line the air fryer basket with baking paper and spray lightly with oil. 2. In a large bowl, toss together the broccoli, peanut oil, garlic, and salt until evenly coated. 3. Spread out the broccoli in an even layer in the prepared basket. 4. Air fry at 204ºC for 15 minutes, stirring halfway through. Make the Sauce: 5. Meanwhile, in a small microwave-safe bowl, combine the soy sauce, honey, Sriracha, and rice vinegar and microwave on high for about 15 seconds. Stir to combine. 6. Transfer the broccoli to a serving bowl and add the sauce. Gently toss until evenly coated and serve immediately.

Butternut Squash Croquettes

Prep time: 5 minutes | Cook time: 17 minutes | Serves 4

⅓ butternut squash, peeled and grated
40 g plain flour
2 eggs, whisked
4 cloves garlic, minced
1½ tablespoons olive oil
1 teaspoon fine sea salt
⅓ teaspoon freshly ground black pepper, or more to taste
⅓ teaspoon dried sage
A pinch of ground allspice

1. Preheat the air fryer to 176ºC. Line the air fryer basket with baking paper. 2. In a mixing bowl, stir together all the ingredients until well combined. 3. Make the squash croquettes: Use a small ice cream scoop to drop tablespoonful's of the squash mixture onto a lightly floured surface and shape into balls with your hands. Transfer them to the air fryer basket. 4. Air fry for 17 minutes until the squash croquettes are golden brown. 5. Remove from the basket to a plate and serve warm.

Dinner Rolls

Prep time: 10 minutes | Cook time: 12 minutes | Serves 6

125 g shredded Mozzarella cheese
30 g full-fat cream cheese
125 g blanched finely ground almond flour
30 g ground flaxseed
½ teaspoon baking powder
1 large egg

1. Place Mozzarella, cream cheese, and almond flour in a large microwave-safe bowl. Microwave for 1 minute. Mix until smooth. 2. Add flaxseed, baking powder, and egg until fully combined and smooth. Microwave an additional 15 seconds if it becomes too firm. 3. Separate the dough into six pieces and roll into balls. Place the balls into the air fryer basket. 4. Adjust the temperature to 160°C and air fry for 12 minutes. 5. Allow rolls to cool completely before serving.

Spicy Roasted Bok Choy

Prep time: 10 minutes | Cook time: 7 to 10 minutes | Serves 4

2 tablespoons olive oil
2 tablespoons reduced-sodium coconut aminos or tamari
2 teaspoons sesame oil
2 teaspoons chilli garlic sauce
2 cloves garlic, minced
1 head (about 455 g) bok choy, sliced lengthwise into quarters
2 teaspoons black sesame seeds

1. Preheat the air fryer to 204°C. 2. In a large bowl, combine the olive oil, coconut aminos, sesame oil, chilli garlic sauce, and garlic. Add the bok choy and toss, massaging the leaves with your hands if necessary, until thoroughly coated. 3. Arrange the bok choy in the basket of the air fryer. Pausing about halfway through the cooking time to shake the basket, air fry for 7 to 10 minutes until the bok choy is tender and the tips of the leaves begin to crisp. 4. Remove from the basket and let cool for a few minutes before coarsely chopping. Serve sprinkled with the sesame seeds.

Tingly Chilli-Roasted Broccoli

Prep time: 5 minutes | Cook time: 10 minutes | Serves 2

340 g broccoli florets
2 tablespoons Asian hot chilli oil
1 teaspoon ground Sichuan peppercorns (or black pepper)
2 garlic cloves, finely chopped
1 (2-inch) piece fresh ginger, peeled and finely chopped
Kosher or coarse sea salt and freshly ground black pepper, to taste

1. In a bowl, toss together the broccoli, chilli oil, Sichuan peppercorns, garlic, ginger, and salt and black pepper to taste. 2. Transfer to the air fryer and roast at 192°C, shaking the basket halfway through, until lightly charred and tender, about 10 minutes. Remove from the air fryer and serve warm.

Sesame Carrots and Sugar Snap Peas

Prep time: 10 minutes | Cook time: 16 minutes | Serves 4

455 g carrots, peeled sliced on the bias (½-inch slices)
1 teaspoon olive oil
Salt and freshly ground black pepper, to taste
80 g honey
1 tablespoon sesame oil
1 tablespoon soy sauce
½ teaspoon minced fresh ginger
110 g sugar snap peas
1½ teaspoons sesame seeds

1. Preheat the air fryer to 184°C. 2. Toss the carrots with the olive oil, season with salt and pepper and air fry for 10 minutes, shaking the basket once or twice during the cooking process. 3. Combine the honey, sesame oil, soy sauce and minced ginger in a large bowl. Add the sugar snap peas and the air-fried carrots to the honey mixture, toss to coat and return everything to the air fryer basket. 4. Turn up the temperature to 204°C and air fry for an additional 6 minutes, shaking the basket once during the cooking process. 5. Transfer the carrots and sugar snap peas to a serving bowl. Pour the sauce from the bottom of the cooker over the vegetables and sprinkle sesame seeds over top. Serve immediately.

Chapter 4 Poultry

Chicken Breasts with Asparagus, Beans, and Rocket

Prep time: 20 minutes | Cook time: 25 minutes | Serves 2

125 g canned cannellini beans, rinsed
1½ tablespoons red wine vinegar
1 garlic clove, minced
2 tablespoons extra-virgin olive oil, divided
Salt and ground black pepper, to taste
½ red onion, sliced thinly
230 g asparagus, trimmed and cut into 1-inch lengths
2 (230 g) boneless, skinless chicken breasts, trimmed
¼ teaspoon paprika
½ teaspoon ground coriander
60 g baby rocket, rinsed and drained

1. Preheat the air fryer to 204ºC. 2. Warm the beans in microwave for 1 minutes and combine with red wine vinegar, garlic, 1 tablespoon of olive oil, ¼ teaspoon of salt, and ¼ teaspoon of ground black pepper in a bowl. Stir to mix well. 3. Combine the onion with ⅛ teaspoon of salt, ⅛ teaspoon of ground black pepper, and 2 teaspoons of olive oil in a separate bowl. Toss to coat well. 4. Place the onion in the air fryer and air fry for 2 minutes, then add the asparagus and air fry for 8 more minutes or until the asparagus is tender. Shake the basket halfway through. Transfer the onion and asparagus to the bowl with beans. Set aside. 5. Toss the chicken breasts with remaining ingredients, except for the baby arugula, in a large bowl. 6. Put the chicken breasts in the air fryer and air fry for 14 minutes or until the internal temperature of the chicken reaches at least 76ºC. Flip the breasts halfway through. 7. Remove the chicken from the air fryer and serve on an aluminum foil with asparagus, beans, onion, and rocket. Sprinkle with salt and ground black pepper. Toss to serve.

Crisp Paprika Chicken Drumsticks

Prep time: 5 minutes | Cook time: 22 minutes | Serves 2

2 teaspoons paprika
1 teaspoon packed brown sugar
1 teaspoon garlic powder
½ teaspoon dry mustard
½ teaspoon salt
Pinch pepper
4 (140 g) chicken drumsticks, trimmed
1 teaspoon vegetable oil
1 spring onion, green part only, sliced thin on bias

1. Preheat the air fryer to 204ºC. 2. Combine paprika, sugar, garlic powder, mustard, salt, and pepper in a bowl. Pat drumsticks dry with paper towels. Using metal skewer, poke 10 to 15 holes in skin of each drumstick. Rub with oil and sprinkle evenly with spice mixture. 3. Arrange drumsticks in air fryer basket, spaced evenly apart, alternating ends. Air fry until chicken is crisp and registers 92ºC, 22 to 25 minutes, flipping chicken halfway through cooking. 4. Transfer chicken to serving platter, tent loosely with aluminum foil, and let rest for 5 minutes. Sprinkle with spring onion and serve.

Thai-Style Cornish Game Hens

Prep time: 30 minutes | Cook time: 20 minutes | Serves 4

20 g chopped fresh coriander leaves and stems
60 g fish sauce
1 tablespoon soy sauce
1 Serrano chilli, seeded and chopped
8 garlic cloves, smashed
2 tablespoons sugar
2 tablespoons lemongrass paste
2 teaspoons black pepper
2 teaspoons ground coriander
1 teaspoon kosher or coarse sea salt
1 teaspoon ground turmeric
2 Cornish game hens, giblets removed, split in half lengthwise

1. In a blender, combine the coriander, fish sauce, soy sauce, Serrano, garlic, sugar, lemongrass, black pepper, coriander, salt, and turmeric. Blend until smooth. 2. Place the game hen halves in a large bowl. Pour the cilantro mixture over the hen halves and toss to coat. Marinate at room temperature for 30 minutes, or cover and refrigerate for up to 24 hours. 3. Arrange the hen halves in a single layer in the air fryer basket. Set the air fryer to 204ºC for 20 minutes. Use a meat thermometer to ensure the game hens have reached an internal temperature of 76ºC.

Bacon Lovers' Stuffed Chicken

Prep time: 10 minutes | Cook time: 20 minutes | Serves 4

4 (140 g) boneless, skinless chicken breasts, pounded to ¼ inch thick
2 (150 g) packages Boursin cheese (or Kite Hill brand chive cream cheese style spread, softened, for dairy-free)
8 slices thin-cut bacon
Sprig of fresh coriander, for garnish (optional)

1. Spray the air fryer basket with avocado oil. Preheat the air fryer to 204ºC. 2. Place one of the chicken breasts on a cutting board. With a sharp knife held parallel to the cutting board, make a 1-inch-wide incision at the top of the breast. Carefully cut into the breast to form a large pocket, leaving a ½-inch border along the sides and bottom. Repeat with the other 3 chicken breasts. 3. Snip the corner of a large sandwich bag to form a ¾-inch hole. Place the Boursin cheese in the bag and pipe the cheese into the pockets in the chicken breasts, dividing the cheese evenly among them. 4. Wrap 2 slices of bacon around each chicken breast and secure the ends with toothpicks. Place the bacon-wrapped chicken in the air fryer basket and air fry until the bacon is crisp and the chicken's internal temperature reaches 76ºC, about 18 to 20 minutes, flipping after 10 minutes. Garnish with a sprig of coriander before serving, if desired. 5. Store leftovers in an airtight container in the refrigerator for up to 4 days. Reheat in a preheated 204ºC air fryer for 5 minutes, or until warmed through.

Yellow Curry Chicken Thighs with Peanuts

Prep time: 10 minutes | Cook time: 20 minutes | Serves 6

125 ml unsweetened full-fat coconut milk
2 tablespoons yellow curry paste
1 tablespoon minced fresh ginger
1 tablespoon minced garlic
1 teaspoon kosher or coarse sea salt
455 g boneless, skinless chicken thighs, halved crosswise
2 tablespoons chopped peanuts

1. In a large bowl, stir together the coconut milk, curry paste, ginger, garlic, and salt until well blended. Add the chicken; toss well to coat. Marinate at room temperature for 30 minutes, or cover and refrigerate for up to 24 hours. 2. Preheat the air fryer to 192°C. 3. Place the chicken (along with marinade) in a baking pan. Place the pan in the air fryer basket. Bake for 20 minutes, turning the chicken halfway through the cooking time. Use a meat thermometer to ensure the chicken has reached an internal temperature of 76°C. 4. Sprinkle the chicken with the chopped peanuts and serve.

Jalapeño Popper Hasselback Chicken

Prep time: 10 minutes | Cook time: 19 minutes | Serves 2

Oil, for spraying
2 (230 g) boneless, skinless chicken breasts
60 g cream cheese, softened
30 g bacon bits
30 g chopped pickled jalapeños
60 g shredded Cheddar cheese, divided

1. Line the air fryer basket with baking paper and spray lightly with oil. 2. Make multiple cuts across the top of each chicken breast, cutting only halfway through. 3. In a medium bowl, mix together the cream cheese, bacon bits, jalapeños, and 30 g Cheddar cheese. Spoon some of the mixture into each cut. 4. Place the chicken in the prepared basket. 5. Air fry at 176°C for 14 minutes. Scatter the remaining 30 g cheese on top of the chicken and cook for another 2 to 5 minutes, or until the cheese is melted and the internal temperature reaches 76°C.

Mediterranean Stuffed Chicken Breasts

Prep time: 5 minutes | Cook time: 20 to 25 minutes | Serves 4

4 small boneless, skinless chicken breast halves (about 680 g)
Salt and freshly ground black pepper, to taste
110 g goat cheese
6 pitted Kalamata olives, coarsely chopped
Zest of ½ lemon
1 teaspoon minced fresh rosemary or ½ teaspoon ground dried rosemary
60 g almond meal
65 ml balsamic vinegar
6 tablespoons unsalted butter

1. Preheat the air fryer to 184°C. 2. With a boning knife, cut a wide pocket into the thickest part of each chicken breast half, taking care not to cut all the way through. Season the chicken evenly on both sides with salt and freshly ground black pepper. 3. In a small bowl, mix the cheese, olives, lemon zest, and rosemary. Stuff the pockets with the cheese mixture and secure with toothpicks. 4. Place the almond meal in a shallow bowl and dredge the chicken, shaking off the excess. Coat lightly with olive oil spray. 5. Working in batches if necessary, arrange the chicken breasts in a single layer in the air fryer basket. Pausing halfway through the cooking time to flip the chicken, air fry for 20 to 25 minutes, until a thermometer inserted into the thickest part registers 76°C. 6. While the chicken is baking, prepare the sauce. In a small pan over medium heat, simmer the balsamic vinegar until thick and syrupy, about 5 minutes. Set aside until the chicken is done. When ready to serve, warm the sauce over medium heat and whisk in the butter, 1 tablespoon at a time, until melted and smooth. Season to taste with salt and pepper. 7. Serve the chicken breasts with the sauce drizzled on top.

Turkey Meatloaf

Prep time: 10 minutes | Cook time: 50 minutes | Serves 4

230 g sliced mushrooms
1 small onion, coarsely chopped
2 cloves garlic
680 g 85% lean minced turkey
2 eggs, lightly beaten
1 tablespoon tomato paste
30 g almond meal
2 tablespoons almond milk
1 tablespoon dried oregano
1 teaspoon salt
½ teaspoon freshly ground black pepper
1 plum tomato, thinly sliced

1. Preheat the air fryer to 176°C. Lightly coat a round pan with olive oil and set aside. 2. In a food processor fitted with a metal blade, combine the mushrooms, onion, and garlic. Pulse until finely chopped. Transfer the vegetables to a large mixing bowl. 3. Add the turkey, eggs, tomato paste, almond meal, milk, oregano, salt, and black pepper. Mix gently until thoroughly combined. Transfer the mixture to the prepared pan and shape into a loaf. Arrange the tomato slices on top. 4. Air fry for 50 minutes or until the meatloaf is nicely browned and a thermometer inserted into the thickest part registers 76°C. Remove from the air fryer and let rest for about 10 minutes before slicing.

Breaded Turkey Cutlets

Prep time: 5 minutes | Cook time: 8 minutes | Serves 4

60 g whole wheat bread crumbs
¼ teaspoon paprika
¼ teaspoon salt
¼ teaspoon black pepper
⅛ teaspoon dried sage
⅛ teaspoon garlic powder
1 egg
4 turkey breast cutlets
Chopped fresh parsley, for serving

1. Preheat the air fryer to 192°C. 2. In a medium shallow bowl, whisk together the bread crumbs, paprika, salt, black pepper, sage, and garlic powder. 3. In a separate medium shallow bowl, whisk the egg until frothy. 4. Dip each turkey cutlet into the egg mixture, then into the bread crumb mixture, coating the outside with the crumbs. Place the breaded turkey cutlets in a single layer in the bottom of the air fryer basket, making sure that they don't touch each other. 5. Bake for 4 minutes. Turn the cutlets over, then bake for 4 minutes more, or until the internal temperature reaches 76°C. Sprinkle on the parsley and serve.

Quick Chicken Fajitas

Prep time: 10 minutes | Cook time: 15 minutes | Serves 2

280 g boneless, skinless chicken breast, sliced into ¼-inch strips
2 tablespoons coconut oil, melted
1 tablespoon chilli powder
½ teaspoon cumin
½ teaspoon paprika
½ teaspoon garlic powder
¼ medium onion, peeled and sliced
½ medium green bell pepper, seeded and sliced
½ medium red bell pepper, seeded and sliced

1. Place chicken and coconut oil into a large bowl and sprinkle with chilli powder, cumin, paprika, and garlic powder. Toss chicken until well coated with seasoning. Place chicken into the air fryer basket. 2. Adjust the temperature to 176°C and air fry for 15 minutes. 3. Add onion and peppers into the basket when the cooking time has 7 minutes remaining. 4. Toss the chicken two or three times during cooking. Vegetables should be tender and chicken fully cooked to at least 76°C internal temperature when finished. Serve warm.

Sweet and Spicy Turkey Meatballs

Prep time: 15 minutes | Cook time: 15 minutes | Serves 6

Olive oil
455 g lean minced turkey
60 g whole-wheat panko bread crumbs
1 egg, beaten
1 tablespoon soy sauce
80 g hoisin sauce, divided
2 teaspoons minced garlic
⅛ teaspoon salt
⅛ teaspoon freshly ground black pepper
1 teaspoon Sriracha

1. Spray the air fryer basket lightly with olive oil. 2. In a large bowl, mix together the turkey, panko bread crumbs, egg, soy sauce, 1 tablespoon of hoisin sauce, garlic, salt, and black pepper. 3. Using a tablespoon, form 24 meatballs. 4. In a small bowl, combine the remaining 60 g hoisin sauce and Sriracha to make a glaze and set aside. 5. Place the meatballs in the air fryer basket in a single layer. You may need to cook them in batches. 6. Air fry at 176°C for 8 minutes. Brush the meatballs generously with the glaze and cook until cooked through, an additional 4 to 7 minutes.

Chicken Nuggets

Prep time: 10 minutes | Cook time: 15 minutes | Serves 4

455 g ground chicken thighs
60 g shredded Mozzarella cheese
1 large egg, whisked
½ teaspoon salt
¼ teaspoon dried oregano
¼ teaspoon garlic powder

1. In a large bowl, combine all ingredients. Form mixture into twenty nugget shapes, about 2 tablespoons each. 2. Place nuggets into ungreased air fryer basket, working in batches if needed. Adjust the temperature to 192°C and air fry for 15 minutes, turning nuggets halfway through cooking. Let cool 5 minutes before serving.

Cajun-Breaded Chicken Bites

Prep time: 10 minutes | Cook time: 12 minutes | Serves 4

455 g boneless, skinless chicken breasts, cut into 1-inch cubes
125 g heavy whipping cream
½ teaspoon salt
¼ teaspoon ground black pepper
30 g plain pork scratchings, finely crushed
30 g unflavored whey protein powder
½ teaspoon Cajun seasoning

1. Place chicken in a medium bowl and pour in cream. Stir to coat. Sprinkle with salt and pepper. 2. In a separate large bowl, combine pork scratchings, protein powder, and Cajun seasoning. Remove chicken from cream, shaking off any excess, and toss in dry mix until fully coated. 3. Place bites into ungreased air fryer basket. Adjust the temperature to 204°C and air fry for 12 minutes, shaking the basket twice during cooking. Bites will be done when golden brown and have an internal temperature of at least 76°C. Serve warm.

Fajita Chicken Strips

Prep time: 10 minutes | Cook time: 15 minutes | Serves 4

455 g boneless, skinless chicken breasts, cut into strips
3 bell peppers, any color, cut into chunks
1 onion, cut into chunks
1 tablespoon olive oil
1 tablespoon fajita seasoning mix
Cooking spray

1. Preheat the air fryer to 188°C. 2. In a large bowl, mix together the chicken, bell peppers, onion, olive oil, and fajita seasoning mix until completely coated. 3. Spray the air fryer basket lightly with cooking spray. 4. Place the chicken and vegetables in the air fryer basket and lightly spray with cooking spray. 5. Air fry for 7 minutes. Shake the basket and air fry for an additional 5 to 8 minutes, until the chicken is cooked through and the veggies are starting to char. 6. Serve warm.

Nice Goulash

Prep time: 5 minutes | Cook time: 17 minutes | Serves 2

2 red bell peppers, chopped
455 g minced chicken
2 medium tomatoes, diced
125 ml chicken stock
Salt and ground black pepper, to taste
Cooking spray

1. Preheat the air fryer to 184°C. Spritz a baking pan with cooking spray. 2. Set the bell pepper in the baking pan and put in the air fry to broil for 5 minutes or until the bell pepper is tender. Shake the basket halfway through. 3. Add the minced chicken and diced tomatoes in the baking pan and stir to mix well. Broil for 6 more minutes or until the chicken is lightly browned. 4. Pour the chicken stock over and sprinkle with salt and ground black pepper. Stir to mix well. Broil for an additional 6 minutes. 5. Serve immediately.

Nacho Chicken Fries

Prep time: 20 minutes | Cook time: 6 to 7 minutes per batch | Serves 4 to 6

455 g chicken breast fillets
Salt, to taste
30 g plain flour
2 eggs
95 g panko bread crumbs
95 g crushed organic nacho cheese tortilla chips
Oil for misting or cooking spray
Seasoning Mix:
1 tablespoon chilli powder
1 teaspoon ground cumin
½ teaspoon garlic powder
½ teaspoon onion powder

1. Stir together all seasonings in a small cup and set aside. 2. Cut chicken tenders in half crosswise, then cut into strips no wider than about ½ inch. 3. Preheat the air fryer to 200°C. 4. Salt chicken to taste. Place strips in large bowl and sprinkle with 1 tablespoon of the seasoning mix. Stir well to distribute seasonings. 5. Add flour to chicken and stir well to coat all sides. 6. Beat eggs together in a shallow dish. 7. In a second shallow dish, combine the panko, crushed chips, and the remaining 2 teaspoons of seasoning mix. 8. Dip chicken strips in eggs, then roll in crumbs. Mist with oil or cooking spray. 9. Chicken strips will cook best if done in two batches. They can be crowded and overlapping a little but not stacked in double or triple layers. 10. Cook for 4 minutes. Shake basket, mist with oil, and cook 2 to 3 more minutes, until chicken juices run clear and outside is crispy. 11. Repeat step 10 to cook remaining chicken fries.

Taco Chicken

Prep time: 10 minutes | Cook time: 23 minutes | Serves 4

2 large eggs
1 tablespoon water
Fine sea salt and ground black pepper, to taste
125 g pork scratchings, finely crushed
1 teaspoon ground cumin
1 teaspoon smoked paprika
4 (140 g) boneless, skinless chicken breasts or thighs, pounded to ¼ inch thick
250 g salsa
110 g shredded Monterey Jack cheese (omit for dairy-free)
Sprig of fresh coriander, for garnish (optional)

1. Spray the air fryer basket with avocado oil. Preheat the air fryer to 204°C. 2. Crack the eggs into a shallow baking dish, add the water and a pinch each of salt and pepper, and whisk to combine. In another shallow baking dish, stir together the pork scratching crumbs, cumin, and paprika until well combined. 3. Season the chicken breasts well on both sides with salt and pepper. Dip 1 chicken breast in the eggs and let any excess drip off, then dredge both sides of the chicken breast in the pork scratching crumb mixture. Spray the breast with avocado oil and place it in the air fryer basket. Repeat with the remaining 3 chicken breasts. 4. Air fry the chicken in the air fryer for 20 minutes, or until the internal temperature reaches 76°C and the breading is golden brown, flipping halfway through. 5. Dollop each chicken breast with 60 g the salsa and top with 110 g cheese. Return the breasts to the air fryer and cook for 3 minutes, or until the cheese is melted. Garnish with coriander before serving, if desired. 6. Store leftovers in an airtight container in the refrigerator for up to 4 days. Reheat in a preheated 204°C air fryer for 5 minutes, or until warmed through.

Smoky Chicken Leg Quarters

Prep time: 30 minutes | Cook time: 23 to 27 minutes | Serves 6

125 ml avocado oil
2 teaspoons smoked paprika
1 teaspoon sea salt
1 teaspoon garlic powder
½ teaspoon dried rosemary
½ teaspoon dried thyme
½ teaspoon freshly ground black pepper
910 g bone-in, skin-on chicken leg quarters

1. In a blender or small bowl, combine the avocado oil, smoked paprika, salt, garlic powder, rosemary, thyme, and black pepper. 2. Place the chicken in a shallow dish or large sandwich bag. Pour the marinade over the chicken, making sure all the legs are coated. Cover and marinate for at least 2 hours or overnight. 3. Place the chicken in a single layer in the air fryer basket, working in batches if necessary. Set the air fryer to 204°C and air fry for 15 minutes. Flip the chicken legs, then reduce the temperature to 176°C. Cook for 8 to 12 minutes more, until an instant-read thermometer reads 72°C when inserted into the thickest piece of chicken. 4. Allow to rest for 5 to 10 minutes before serving.

General Tso's Chicken

Prep time: 10 minutes | Cook time: 14 minutes | Serves 4

1 tablespoon sesame oil
1 teaspoon minced garlic
½ teaspoon ground ginger
250 ml chicken stock
4 tablespoons soy sauce, divided
½ teaspoon Sriracha, plus more for serving
2 tablespoons hoisin sauce
4 tablespoons cornflour, divided
4 boneless, skinless chicken breasts, cut into 1-inch pieces
Olive oil spray
2 medium spring onions, sliced, green parts only
Sesame seeds, for garnish

1. In a small saucepan over low heat, combine the sesame oil, garlic, and ginger and cook for 1 minute. 2. Add the chicken stock, 2 tablespoons of soy sauce, the Sriracha, and hoisin. Whisk to combine. 3. Whisk in 2 tablespoons of cornflour and continue cooking over low heat until the sauce starts to thicken, about 5 minutes. Remove the pan from the heat, cover it, and set aside. 4. Insert the crisper plate into the basket and the basket into the unit. Preheat the unit by selecting BAKE, setting the temperature to 204°C, and setting the time to 3 minutes. Select START/STOP to begin. 5. In a medium bowl, toss together the chicken, remaining 2 tablespoons of soy sauce, and remaining 2 tablespoons of cornflour. 6. Once the unit is preheated, spray the crisper plate with olive oil. Place the chicken into the basket and spray it with olive oil. 7. Select BAKE, set the temperature to 204°C, and set the time to 9 minutes. Select START/STOP to begin. 8. After 5 minutes, remove the basket, shake, and spray the chicken with more olive oil. Reinsert the basket to resume cooking. 9. When the cooking is complete, a food thermometer inserted into the chicken should register at least 76°C. Transfer the chicken to a large bowl and toss it with the sauce. Garnish with the spring onions and sesame seeds and serve.

Bacon-Wrapped Stuffed Chicken Breasts

Prep time: 15 minutes | Cook time: 30 minutes | Serves 4

10 g chopped frozen spinach, thawed and squeezed dry	1 teaspoon black pepper
30 g cream cheese, softened	2 large boneless, skinless chicken breasts, butterflied and pounded to ½-inch thickness
30 g grated Parmesan cheese	
1 jalapeño, seeded and chopped	4 teaspoons salt-free Cajun seasoning
½ teaspoon kosher or coarse sea salt	6 slices bacon

1. In a small bowl, combine the spinach, cream cheese, Parmesan cheese, jalapeño, salt, and pepper. Stir until well combined. 2. Place the butterflied chicken breasts on a flat surface. Spread the cream cheese mixture evenly across each piece of chicken. Starting with the narrow end, roll up each chicken breast, ensuring the filling stays inside. Season chicken with the Cajun seasoning, patting it in to ensure it sticks to the meat. 3. Wrap each breast in 3 slices of bacon. Place in the air fryer basket. Set the air fryer to 176°C for 30 minutes. Use a meat thermometer to ensure the chicken has reached an internal temperature of 76°C. 4. Let the chicken stand 5 minutes before slicing each rolled-up breast in half to serve.

Golden Chicken Cutlets

Prep time: 15 minutes | Cook time: 15 minutes | Serves 4

2 tablespoons panko breadcrumbs	4 chicken cutlets
30 g grated Parmesan cheese	1 tablespoon parsley
⅛ tablespoon paprika	Salt and ground black pepper, to taste
½ tablespoon garlic powder	Cooking spray
2 large eggs	

1. Preheat air fryer to 204°C. Spritz the air fryer basket with cooking spray. 2. Combine the breadcrumbs, Parmesan, paprika, garlic powder, salt, and ground black pepper in a large bowl. Stir to mix well. Beat the eggs in a separate bowl. 3. Dredge the chicken cutlets in the beaten eggs, then roll over the breadcrumbs mixture to coat well. Shake the excess off. 4. Transfer the chicken cutlets in the preheated air fryer and spritz with cooking spray. 5. Air fry for 15 minutes or until crispy and golden brown. Flip the cutlets halfway through. 6. Serve with parsley on top.

Pork Scratching Fried Chicken

Prep time: 30 minutes | Cook time: 20 minutes | Serves 4

60 g buffalo sauce	½ teaspoon garlic powder
4 (110 g) boneless, skinless chicken breasts	¼ teaspoon ground black pepper
½ teaspoon paprika	60 g pork scratchings, finely crushed

1. Pour buffalo sauce into a large sealable bowl or bag. Add chicken and toss to coat. Place sealed bowl or bag into refrigerator and let marinate at least 30 minutes up to overnight. 2. Remove chicken from marinade but do not shake excess sauce off chicken. Sprinkle both sides of thighs with paprika, garlic powder, and pepper. 3. Place pork scratchings into a large bowl and press each chicken breast into scratchings to coat evenly on both sides. 4. Place chicken into ungreased air fryer basket. Adjust the temperature to 204°C and roast for 20 minutes, turning chicken halfway through cooking. Chicken will be golden and have an internal temperature of at least 76°C when done. Serve warm.

Porchetta-Style Chicken Breasts

Prep time: 10 minutes | Cook time: 15 minutes | Serves 4

10 g fresh parsley leaves	1 teaspoon ground fennel
5 g roughly chopped fresh chives	½ teaspoon red pepper flakes
4 cloves garlic, peeled	4 (110 g) boneless, skinless chicken breasts, pounded to ¼ inch thick
2 tablespoons lemon juice	
3 teaspoons fine sea salt	8 slices bacon
1 teaspoon dried rubbed sage	Sprigs of fresh rosemary, for garnish (optional)
1 teaspoon fresh rosemary leaves	

1. Spray the air fryer basket with avocado oil. Preheat the air fryer to 172°C. 2. Place the parsley, chives, garlic, lemon juice, salt, sage, rosemary, fennel, and red pepper flakes in a food processor and purée until a smooth paste forms. 3. Place the chicken breasts on a cutting board and rub the paste all over the tops. With a short end facing you, roll each breast up like a jelly roll to make a log and secure it with toothpicks. 4. Wrap 2 slices of bacon around each chicken breast log to cover the entire breast. Secure the bacon with toothpicks. 5. Place the chicken breast logs in the air fryer basket and air fry for 5 minutes, flip the logs over, and cook for another 5 minutes. Increase the heat to 200°C and cook until the bacon is crisp, about 5 minutes more. 6. Remove the toothpicks and garnish with fresh rosemary sprigs, if desired, before serving. Store leftovers in an airtight container in the refrigerator for up to 4 days or in the freezer for up to a month. Reheat in a preheated 176°C air fryer for 5 minutes, then increase the heat to 200°C and cook for 2 minutes to crisp the bacon.

Ethiopian Chicken with Cauliflower

Prep time: 15 minutes | Cook time: 28 minutes | Serves 6

2 handful fresh Italian parsley, roughly chopped	⅓ teaspoon porcini powder
10 g fresh chopped chives	1½ teaspoons berbere spice
2 sprigs thyme	⅓ teaspoon sweet paprika
6 chicken drumsticks	½ teaspoon shallot powder
1½ small-sized head cauliflower, broken into large-sized florets	1 teaspoon granulated garlic
	1 teaspoon freshly cracked pink peppercorns
2 teaspoons mustard powder	½ teaspoon sea salt

1. Simply combine all items for the berbere spice rub mix. After that, coat the chicken drumsticks with this rub mix on all sides. Transfer them to the baking dish. 2. Now, lower the cauliflower onto the chicken drumsticks. Add thyme, chives and Italian parsley and spritz everything with a pan spray. Transfer the baking dish to the preheated air fryer. 3. Next step, set the timer for 28 minutes; roast at 180°C, turning occasionally. Bon appétit!

Crunchy Chicken with Roasted Carrots

Prep time: 10 minutes | Cook time: 22 minutes | Serves 4

4 bone-in, skin-on chicken thighs
2 carrots, cut into 2-inch pieces
2 tablespoons extra-virgin olive oil
2 teaspoons poultry spice
1 teaspoon sea salt, divided
2 teaspoons chopped fresh rosemary leaves
Cooking oil spray
250 g cooked white rice

1. Brush the chicken thighs and carrots with olive oil. Sprinkle both with the poultry spice, salt, and rosemary. 2. Insert the crisper plate into the basket and the basket into the unit. Preheat the unit by selecting AIR FRY, setting the temperature to 204ºC, and setting the time to 3 minutes. Select START/STOP to begin. 3. Once the unit is preheated, spray the crisper plate with cooking oil. Place the carrots into the basket. Add the wire rack and arrange the chicken thighs on the rack. 4. Select AIR FRY, set the temperature to 204ºC, and set the time to 20 minutes. Select START/STOP to begin. 5. When the cooking is complete, check the chicken temperature. If a food thermometer inserted into the chicken registers 76ºC, remove the chicken from the air fryer, place it on a clean plate, and cover with aluminum foil to keep warm. Otherwise, resume cooking for 1 to 2 minutes longer. 6. The carrots can cook for 18 to 22 minutes and will be tender and caramelised; cooking time isn't as crucial for root vegetables. 7. Serve the chicken and carrots with the hot cooked rice.

Blackened Cajun Chicken Tenders

Prep time: 10 minutes | Cook time: 17 minutes | Serves 4

2 teaspoons paprika
1 teaspoon chilli powder
½ teaspoon garlic powder
½ teaspoon dried thyme
¼ teaspoon onion powder
⅛ teaspoon ground cayenne pepper
2 tablespoons coconut oil
455 g boneless, skinless chicken breast fillets
60 g full-fat ranch dressing

1. In a small bowl, combine all seasonings. 2. Drizzle oil over chicken fillets and then generously coat each tender in the spice mixture. Place fillets into the air fryer basket. 3. Adjust the temperature to 192ºC and air fry for 17 minutes. 4. Fillets will be 76ºC internally when fully cooked. Serve with ranch dressing for dipping.

Coriander Chicken Kebabs

Prep time: 30 minutes | Cook time: 10 minutes | Serves 4

Chutney:
60 g unsweetened desiccated coconut
125 ml hot water
40 g fresh coriander leaves, roughly chopped
5 g fresh mint leaves, roughly chopped
6 cloves garlic, roughly chopped
1 jalapeño, seeded and roughly chopped
180 ml water, as needed
Juice of 1 lemon
Chicken:
455 g boneless, skinless chicken thighs, cut crosswise into thirds
Olive oil spray

1. For the chutney: In a blender or food processor, combine the coconut and hot water; set aside to soak for 5 minutes. 2. To the processor, add the coriander, mint, garlic, and jalapeño, along with 65 ml water. Blend at low speed, stopping occasionally to scrape down the sides. Add the lemon juice. With the blender or processor running, add only enough additional water to keep the contents moving. Turn the blender to high once the contents are moving freely and blend until the mixture is puréed. 3. For the chicken: Place the chicken pieces in a large bowl. Add 60 g chutney and mix well to coat. Set aside the remaining chutney to use as a dip. Marinate the chicken for 15 minutes at room temperature. 4. Spray the air fryer basket with olive oil spray. Arrange the chicken in the air fryer basket. Set the air fryer to 176ºC for 10 minutes. Use a meat thermometer to ensure that the chicken has reached an internal temperature of 76ºC. 5. Serve the chicken with the remaining chutney.

Lemon Thyme Roasted Chicken

Prep time: 10 minutes | Cook time: 60 minutes | Serves 6

1 (1.8 kg) chicken
2 teaspoons dried thyme
1 teaspoon garlic powder
½ teaspoon onion powder
2 teaspoons dried parsley
1 teaspoon baking powder
1 medium lemon
2 tablespoons salted butter, melted

1. Rub chicken with thyme, garlic powder, onion powder, parsley, and baking powder. 2. Slice lemon and place four slices on top of chicken, breast side up, and secure with toothpicks. Place remaining slices inside of the chicken. 3. Place entire chicken into the air fryer basket, breast side down. 4. Adjust the temperature to 176ºC and air fry for 60 minutes. 5. After 30 minutes, flip chicken so breast side is up. 6. When done, internal temperature should be 76ºC and the skin golden and crispy. To serve, pour melted butter over entire chicken.

Chicken Schnitzel

Prep time: 15 minutes | Cook time: 5 minutes | Serves 4

60 g plain flour
1 teaspoon marjoram
½ teaspoon thyme
1 teaspoon dried parsley flakes
½ teaspoon salt
1 egg
1 teaspoon lemon juice
1 teaspoon water
125 g breadcrumbs
4 chicken breast fillets, pounded thin, cut in half lengthwise
Cooking spray

1. Preheat the air fryer to 200ºC and spritz with cooking spray. 2. Combine the flour, marjoram, thyme, parsley, and salt in a shallow dish. Stir to mix well. 3. Whisk the egg with lemon juice and water in a large bowl. Pour the breadcrumbs in a separate shallow dish. 4. Roll the chicken halves in the flour mixture first, then in the egg mixture, and then roll over the breadcrumbs to coat well. Shake the excess off. 5. Arrange the chicken halves in the preheated air fryer and spritz with cooking spray on both sides. 6. Air fry for 5 minutes or until the chicken halves are golden brown and crispy. Flip the halves halfway through. 7. Serve immediately.

Chapter 5 Fish and Seafood

New Orleans-Style Crab Cakes

Prep time: 10 minutes | Cook time: 8 to 10 minutes | Serves 4

160 g bread crumbs
2 teaspoons Creole Seasoning
1 teaspoon dry mustard
1 teaspoon salt
1 teaspoon freshly ground black pepper
185 g crab meat
2 large eggs, beaten
1 teaspoon butter, melted
40 g minced onion
Cooking spray
Pecan Tartar Sauce, for serving

1. Preheat the air fryer to 176°C. Line the air fryer basket with baking paper. 2. In a medium bowl, whisk the bread crumbs, Creole Seasoning, dry mustard, salt, and pepper until blended. Add the crab meat, eggs, butter, and onion. Stir until blended. Shape the crab mixture into 8 patties. 3. Place the crab cakes on the baking paper and spritz with oil. 4. Air fry for 4 minutes. Flip the cakes, spritz them with oil, and air fry for 4 to 6 minutes more until the outsides are firm and a fork inserted into the center comes out clean. Serve with the Pecan Tartar Sauce.

Apple Cider Mussels

Prep time: 10 minutes | Cook time: 2 minutes | Serves 5

910 g mussels, cleaned and debearded
1 teaspoon onion powder
1 teaspoon ground cumin
1 tablespoon avocado oil
65 ml apple cider vinegar

1. Mix mussels with onion powder, ground cumin, avocado oil, and apple cider vinegar. 2. Put the mussels in the air fryer and cook at 200°C for 2 minutes.

Crab-Stuffed Avocado Boats

Prep time: 5 minutes | Cook time: 7 minutes | Serves 4

2 medium avocados, halved and pitted
230 g cooked crab meat
¼ teaspoon Old Bay seasoning
2 tablespoons peeled and diced yellow onion
2 tablespoons mayonnaise

1. Scoop out avocado flesh in each avocado half, leaving ½ inch around edges to form a shell. Chop scooped-out avocado. 2. In a medium bowl, combine crab meat, Old Bay seasoning, onion, mayonnaise, and chopped avocado. Place ¼ mixture into each avocado shell. 3. Place avocado boats into ungreased air fryer basket. Adjust the temperature to 176°C and air fry for 7 minutes. Avocado will be browned on the top and mixture will be bubbling when done. Serve warm.

Tuna and Fruit Kebabs

Prep time: 15 minutes | Cook time: 8 to 12 minutes | Serves 4

455 g tuna steaks, cut into 1-inch cubes
60 g canned pineapple chunks, drained, juice reserved
60 g large red grapes
1 tablespoon honey
2 teaspoons grated fresh ginger
1 teaspoon olive oil
Pinch cayenne pepper

1. Thread the tuna, pineapple, and grapes on 8 bamboo or 4 metal skewers that fit in the air fryer. 2. In a small bowl, whisk the honey, 1 tablespoon of reserved pineapple juice, the ginger, olive oil, and cayenne. Brush this mixture over the kebabs. Let them stand for 10 minutes. 3. Air fry the kebabs at 188°C for 8 to 12 minutes, or until the tuna reaches an internal temperature of at least 64°C on a meat thermometer, and the fruit is tender and glazed, brushing once with the remaining sauce. Discard any remaining marinade. Serve immediately.

White Fish with Cauliflower

Prep time: 30 minutes | Cook time: 13 minutes | Serves 4

230 g cauliflower florets
½ teaspoon English mustard
2 tablespoons butter, room temperature
½ tablespoon coriander, minced
2 tablespoons sour cream
310 g cooked white fish
Salt and freshly cracked black pepper, to taste

1. Boil the cauliflower until tender. Then, purée the cauliflower in your blender. Transfer to a mixing dish. 2. Now, stir in the fish, coriander, salt, and black pepper. 3. Add the sour cream, English mustard, and butter; mix until everything's well incorporated. Using your hands, shape into patties. 4. Place in the refrigerator for about 2 hours. Cook for 13 minutes at 200°C. Serve with some extra English mustard.

Pesto Prawns with Wild Rice Pilaf

Prep time: 5 minutes | Cook time: 5 minutes | Serves 4

455 g medium prawns, peeled and deveined
60 g pesto sauce
1 lemon, sliced
250 g cooked wild rice pilaf

1. Preheat the air fryer to 184°C. 2. In a medium bowl, toss the prawns with the pesto sauce until well coated. 3. Place the prawns in a single layer in the air fryer basket. Put the lemon slices over the prawns and roast for 5 minutes. 4. Remove the lemons and discard. Serve a quarter of the prawns over 60 g wild rice with some favorite steamed vegetables.

Tuna Steak

Prep time: 10 minutes | Cook time: 12 minutes | Serves 4

455 g tuna steaks, boneless and cubed
1 tablespoon mustard
1 tablespoon avocado oil
1 tablespoon apple cider vinegar

1. Mix avocado oil with mustard and apple cider vinegar. 2. Then brush tuna steaks with mustard mixture and put in the air fryer basket. 3. Cook the fish at 184ºC for 6 minutes per side.

Coconut Prawns with Spicy Dipping Sauce

Prep time: 15 minutes | Cook time: 8 minutes | Serves 4

1 (70 g) bag pork scratchings
95 g unsweetened desiccated coconut
95 g coconut flour
1 teaspoon onion powder
1 teaspoon garlic powder
2 eggs
680 g large prawns, peeled and deveined
½ teaspoon salt
¼ teaspoon freshly ground black pepper
Spicy Dipping Sauce:
125 g mayonnaise
2 tablespoons Sriracha
Zest and juice of ½ lime
1 clove garlic, minced

1. Preheat the air fryer to 200ºC. 2. In a food processor fitted with a metal blade, combine the pork scratchings and coconut flakes. Pulse until the mixture resembles coarse crumbs. Transfer to a shallow bowl. 3. In another shallow bowl, combine the coconut flour, onion powder, and garlic powder; mix until thoroughly combined. 4. In a third shallow bowl, whisk the eggs until slightly frothy. 5. In a large bowl, season the prawns with the salt and pepper, tossing gently to coat. 6. Working a few pieces at a time, dredge the prawns in the flour mixture, followed by the eggs, and finishing with the pork scratching crumb mixture. Arrange the prawns on a baking sheet until ready to air fry. 7. Working in batches if necessary, arrange the prawns in a single layer in the air fryer basket. Pausing halfway through the cooking time to turn the prawns, air fry for 8 minutes until cooked through. 8. To make the sauce: In a small bowl, combine the mayonnaise, Sriracha, lime zest and juice, and garlic. Whisk until thoroughly combined. Serve alongside the prawns.

Crawfish Creole Casserole

Prep time: 20 minutes | Cook time: 25 minutes | Serves 4

185 g crawfish meat
60 g chopped celery
60 g chopped onion
60 g chopped green bell pepper
2 large eggs, beaten
250 ml single cream
1 tablespoon butter, melted
1 tablespoon cornflour
1 teaspoon Creole seasoning
¾ teaspoon salt
½ teaspoon freshly ground black pepper
125 g shredded Cheddar cheese
Cooking spray

1. In a medium bowl, stir together the crawfish, celery, onion, and green pepper. 2. In another medium bowl, whisk the eggs, single cream, butter, cornflour, Creole seasoning, salt, and pepper until blended. Stir the egg mixture into the crawfish mixture. Add the cheese and stir to combine. 3. Preheat the air fryer to 148ºC. Spritz a baking pan with oil. 4. Transfer the crawfish mixture to the prepared pan and place it in the air fryer basket. 5. Bake for 25 minutes, stirring every 10 minutes, until a knife inserted into the center comes out clean. 6. Serve immediately.

Breaded Prawn Tacos

Prep time: 10 minutes | Cook time: 9 minutes | Makes 8 tacos

2 large eggs
1 teaspoon prepared yellow mustard
455 g small prawns, peeled, deveined, and tails removed
60 g finely shredded Gouda or Parmesan cheese
60 g pork scratchings, ground to dust
For Serving:
8 large round lettuce leaves
60 g Pico de Gallo
30 g shredded purple cabbage
1 lemon, sliced
Guacamole (optional)

1. Preheat the air fryer to 204ºC. 2. Crack the eggs into a large bowl, add the mustard, and whisk until well combined. Add the prawns and stir well to coat. 3. In a medium-sized bowl, mix together the cheese and pork dust until well combined. 4. One at a time, roll the coated prawns in the pork dust mixture and use your hands to press it onto each prawn. Spray the coated prawns with avocado oil and place them in the air fryer basket, leaving space between them. 5. Air fry the prawns for 9 minutes, or until cooked through and no longer translucent, flipping after 4 minutes. 6. To serve, place a lettuce leaf on a serving plate, place several prawns on top, and top with 1½ teaspoons each of Pico de Gallo and purple cabbage. Squeeze some lemon juice on top and serve with guacamole, if desired. 7. Store leftover prawns in an airtight container in the refrigerator for up to 3 days. Reheat in a preheated 204ºC air fryer for 5 minutes, or until warmed through.

Cod with Avocado

Prep time: 30 minutes | Cook time: 10 minutes | Serves 2

125 g shredded cabbage
60 g full-fat sour cream
2 tablespoons full-fat mayonnaise
30 g chopped pickled jalapeños
2 (85 g) cod fillets
1 teaspoon chilli powder
1 teaspoon cumin
½ teaspoon paprika
¼ teaspoon garlic powder
1 medium avocado, peeled, pitted, and sliced
½ medium lime

1. In a large bowl, place cabbage, sour cream, mayonnaise, and jalapeños. Mix until fully coated. Let sit for 20 minutes in the refrigerator. 2. Sprinkle cod fillets with chilli powder, cumin, paprika, and garlic powder. Place each fillet into the air fryer basket. 3. Adjust the temperature to 188ºC and set the timer for 10 minutes. 4. Flip the fillets halfway through the cooking time. When fully cooked, fish should have an internal temperature of at least 64ºC. 5. To serve, divide slaw mixture into two serving bowls, break cod fillets into pieces and spread over the bowls, and top with avocado. Squeeze lime juice over each bowl. Serve immediately.

Panko-Crusted Fish Sticks

Prep time: 10 minutes | Cook time: 15 minutes | Serves 4

Tartar Sauce:
500 g mayonnaise
2 tablespoons dill pickle relish
1 tablespoon dried minced onions
Fish Sticks:
Oil, for spraying
455 g tilapia fillets
60 g plain flour
250 g panko bread crumbs
2 tablespoons Creole seasoning
2 teaspoons garlic granules
1 teaspoon onion powder
½ teaspoon salt
¼ teaspoon freshly ground black pepper
1 large egg

Make the Tartar Sauce: 1. In a small bowl, whisk together the mayonnaise, pickle relish, and onions. Cover with plastic wrap and refrigerate until ready to serve. You can make this sauce ahead of time; the flavors will intensify as it chills. Make the Fish Sticks: 2. Preheat the air fryer to 176ºC. Line the air fryer basket with baking paper and spray lightly with oil. 3. Cut the fillets into equal-size sticks and place them in a sandwich bag. 4. Add the flour to the bag, seal, and shake well until evenly coated. 5. In a shallow bowl, mix together the bread crumbs, Creole seasoning, garlic, onion powder, salt, and black pepper. 6. In a small bowl, whisk the egg. 7. Dip the fish sticks in the egg, then dredge in the bread crumb mixture until completely coated. 8. Place the fish sticks in the prepared basket. You may need to work in batches, depending on the size of your air fryer. Do not overcrowd. Spray lightly with oil. 9. Cook for 12 to 15 minutes, or until browned and cooked through. Serve with the tartar sauce.

Crab Legs

Prep time: 5 minutes | Cook time: 15 minutes | Serves 4

60 g salted butter, melted and divided
1.4 kg crab legs
¼ teaspoon garlic powder
Juice of ½ medium lemon

1. In a large bowl, drizzle 2 tablespoons butter over crab legs. Place crab legs into the air fryer basket. 2. Adjust the temperature to 204ºC and air fry for 15 minutes. 3. Shake the air fryer basket to toss the crab legs halfway through the cooking time. 4. In a small bowl, mix remaining butter, garlic powder, and lemon juice. 5. To serve, crack open crab legs and remove meat. Dip in lemon butter.

Snapper Scampi

Prep time: 5 minutes | Cook time: 8 to 10 minutes | Serves 4

4 (170 g) skinless snapper or arctic char fillets
1 tablespoon olive oil
3 tablespoons lemon juice, divided
½ teaspoon dried basil
Pinch salt
Freshly ground black pepper, to taste
2 tablespoons butter
2 cloves garlic, minced

1. Rub the fish fillets with olive oil and 1 tablespoon of the lemon juice. Sprinkle with the basil, salt, and pepper, and place in the air fryer basket. 2. Air fry the fish at 192ºC for 7 to 8 minutes or until the fish just flakes when tested with a fork. Remove the fish from the basket and put on a serving plate. Cover to keep warm. 3. In a baking pan, combine the butter, remaining 2 tablespoons lemon juice, and garlic. Bake in the air fryer for 1 to 2 minutes or until the garlic is sizzling. Pour this mixture over the fish and serve

Scallops with Asparagus and Peas

Prep time: 10 minutes | Cook time: 7 to 10 minutes | Serves 4

Cooking oil spray
455 g asparagus, ends trimmed, cut into 2-inch pieces
125 g sugar snap peas
455 g sea scallops
1 tablespoon freshly squeezed
lemon juice
2 teaspoons extra-virgin olive oil
½ teaspoon dried thyme
Salt and freshly ground black pepper, to taste

1. Insert the crisper plate into the basket and the basket into the unit. Preheat the unit by selecting AIR FRY, setting the temperature to 204ºC, and setting the time to 3 minutes. Select START/STOP to begin. 2. Once the unit is preheated, spray the crisper plate with cooking oil. Place the asparagus and sugar snap peas into the basket. 3. Select AIR FRY, set the temperature to 204ºC, and set the time to 10 minutes. Select START/STOP to begin. 4. Meanwhile, check the scallops for a small muscle attached to the side. Pull it off and discard. In a medium bowl, toss together the scallops, lemon juice, olive oil, and thyme. Season with salt and pepper. 5. After 3 minutes, the vegetables should be just starting to get tender. Place the scallops on top of the vegetables. Reinsert the basket to resume cooking. After 3 minutes more, remove the basket and shake it. Again reinsert the basket to resume cooking. 6. When the cooking is complete, the scallops should be firm when tested with your finger and opaque in the center, and the vegetables tender. Serve immediately.

Cajun and Lemon Pepper Cod

Prep time: 5 minutes | Cook time: 12 minutes | Makes 2 cod fillets

1 tablespoon Cajun seasoning
1 teaspoon salt
½ teaspoon lemon pepper
½ teaspoon freshly ground black pepper
2 (230 g) cod fillets, cut to fit
into the air fryer basket
Cooking spray
2 tablespoons unsalted butter, melted
1 lemon, cut into 4 wedges

1. Preheat the air fryer to 184ºC. Spritz the air fryer basket with cooking spray. 2. Thoroughly combine the Cajun seasoning, salt, lemon pepper, and black pepper in a small bowl. Rub this mixture all over the cod fillets until completely coated. 3. Put the fillets in the air fryer basket and brush the melted butter over both sides of each fillet. 4. Bake in the preheated air fryer for 12 minutes, flipping the fillets halfway through, or until the fish flakes easily with a fork. 5. Remove the fillets from the basket and serve with fresh lemon wedges.

Crab Cake Sandwich

Prep time: 15 minutes | Cook time: 10 minutes | Serves 4

Crab Cakes:
60 g panko bread crumbs
1 large egg, beaten
1 large egg white
1 tablespoon mayonnaise
1 teaspoon Dijon mustard
5 g minced fresh parsley
1 tablespoon fresh lemon juice
½ teaspoon Old Bay seasoning
⅛ teaspoon sweet paprika
⅛ teaspoon kosher or coarse sea salt
Freshly ground black pepper, to taste
280 g lump crab meat
Cooking spray
Cajun Mayo:
60 g mayonnaise
1 tablespoon minced dill pickle
1 teaspoon fresh lemon juice
¾ teaspoon Cajun seasoning
For Serving:
4 round lettuce leaves
4 whole wheat potato buns or gluten-free buns

1. For the crab cakes: In a large bowl, combine the panko, whole egg, egg white, mayonnaise, mustard, parsley, lemon juice, Old Bay, paprika, salt, and pepper to taste and mix well. Fold in the crab meat, being careful not to over mix. Gently shape into 4 round patties, about 60 g each, ¾ inch thick. Spray both sides with oil. 2. Preheat the air fryer to 188°C. 3. Working in batches, place the crab cakes in the air fryer basket. Air fry for about 10 minutes, flipping halfway, until the edges are golden. 4. Meanwhile, for the Cajun mayo: In a small bowl, combine the mayonnaise, pickle, lemon juice, and Cajun seasoning. 5. To serve: Place a lettuce leaf on each bun bottom and top with a crab cake and a generous tablespoon of Cajun mayonnaise. Add the bun top and serve.

Classic Prawn Empanadas

Prep time: 10 minutes | Cook time: 8 minutes | Serves 5

230 g raw prawns, peeled, deveined and chopped
30 g chopped red onion
1 spring onion, chopped
2 garlic cloves, minced
2 tablespoons minced red bell pepper
2 tablespoons chopped fresh coriander
½ tablespoon fresh lime juice
¼ teaspoon sweet paprika
⅛ teaspoon kosher or coarse sea salt
⅛ teaspoon crushed red pepper flakes (optional)
1 large egg, beaten
10 frozen Goya Empanada Discs, thawed
Cooking spray

1. In a medium bowl, combine the prawns, red onion, spring onion, garlic, bell pepper, coriander, lime juice, paprika, salt, and pepper flakes (if using). 2. In a small bowl, beat the egg with 1 teaspoon water until smooth. 3. Place an empanada disc on a work surface and put 2 tablespoons of the prawn mixture in the center. Brush the outer edges of the disc with the egg wash. Fold the disc over and gently press the edges to seal. Use a fork and press around the edges to crimp and seal completely. Brush the tops of the empanadas with the egg wash. 4. Preheat the air fryer to 192°C. 5. Spray the bottom of the air fryer basket with cooking spray to prevent sticking. Working in batches, arrange a single layer of the empanadas in the air fryer basket and air fry for about 8 minutes, flipping halfway, until golden brown and crispy. 6. Serve hot.

Parmesan-Crusted Halibut Fillets

Prep time: 5 minutes | Cook time: 10 minutes | Serves 4

2 medium-sized halibut fillets
Dash of tabasco sauce
1 teaspoon curry powder
½ teaspoon ground coriander
½ teaspoon hot paprika
Kosher or coarse sea salt and freshly cracked mixed peppercorns, to taste
2 eggs
1½ tablespoons olive oil
60 g grated Parmesan cheese

1. Preheat the air fryer to 184°C. 2. On a clean work surface, drizzle the halibut fillets with the tabasco sauce. Sprinkle with the curry powder, coriander, hot paprika, salt, and cracked mixed peppercorns. Set aside. 3. In a shallow bowl, beat the eggs until frothy. In another shallow bowl, combine the olive oil and Parmesan cheese. 4. One at a time, dredge the halibut fillets in the beaten eggs, shaking off any excess, then roll them over the Parmesan cheese until evenly coated. 5. Arrange the halibut fillets in the air fryer basket in a single layer and air fry for 10 minutes, or until the fish is golden brown and crisp. 6. Cool for 5 minutes before serving.

Rainbow Salmon Kebabs

Prep time: 10 minutes | Cook time: 8 minutes | Serves 2

170 g boneless, skinless salmon, cut into 1-inch cubes
¼ medium red onion, peeled and cut into 1-inch pieces
½ medium yellow bell pepper, seeded and cut into 1-inch pieces
½ medium courgette, trimmed and cut into ½-inch slices
1 tablespoon olive oil
½ teaspoon salt
¼ teaspoon ground black pepper

1. Using one (6-inch) skewer, skewer 1 piece salmon, then 1 piece onion, 1 piece bell pepper, and finally 1 piece courgette. Repeat this pattern with additional skewers to make four kebabs total. Drizzle with olive oil and sprinkle with salt and black pepper. 2. Place kebabs into ungreased air fryer basket. Adjust the temperature to 204°C and air fry for 8 minutes, turning kebabs halfway through cooking. Salmon will easily flake and have an internal temperature of at least 64°C when done; vegetables will be tender. Serve warm.

Sesame-Crusted Tuna Steak

Prep time: 5 minutes | Cook time: 8 minutes | Serves 2

2 (170 g) tuna steaks
1 tablespoon coconut oil, melted
½ teaspoon garlic powder
2 teaspoons white sesame seeds
2 teaspoons black sesame seeds

1. Brush each tuna steak with coconut oil and sprinkle with garlic powder. 2. In a large bowl, mix sesame seeds and then press each tuna steak into them, covering the steak as completely as possible. Place tuna steaks into the air fryer basket. 3. Adjust the temperature to 204°C and air fry for 8 minutes. 4. Flip the steaks halfway through the cooking time. Steaks will be well-done at 64°C internal temperature. Serve warm.

Chapter 5 Fish and Seafood | 25

Steamed Tuna with Lemongrass

Prep time: 10 minutes | Cook time: 10 minutes | Serves 4

4 small tuna steaks
2 tablespoons low-sodium soy sauce
2 teaspoons sesame oil
2 teaspoons rice wine vinegar
1 teaspoon grated peeled fresh ginger
⅛ teaspoon freshly ground black pepper
1 stalk lemongrass, bent in half
3 tablespoons freshly squeezed lemon juice

1. Place the tuna steaks on a plate. 2. In a small bowl, whisk the soy sauce, sesame oil, vinegar, and ginger until combined. Pour this mixture over the tuna and gently rub it into both sides. Sprinkle the fish with the pepper. Let marinate for 10 minutes. 3. Insert the crisper plate into the basket and the basket into the unit. Preheat the unit by selecting BAKE, setting the temperature to 200ºC, and setting the time to 3 minutes. Select START/STOP to begin. 4. Once the unit is preheated, place the lemongrass into the basket and top it with the tuna steaks. Drizzle the tuna with the lemon juice and 1 tablespoon of water. 5. Select BAKE, set the temperature to 200ºC, and set the time to 10 minutes. Select START/STOP to begin. 6. When the cooking is complete, a food thermometer inserted into the tuna should register at least 64ºC. Discard the lemongrass and serve the tuna.

Creamy Haddock

Prep time: 10 minutes | Cook time: 8 minutes | Serves 4

455 g haddock fillet
1 teaspoon cayenne pepper
1 teaspoon salt
1 teaspoon coconut oil
125 g heavy cream

1. Grease a baking pan with coconut oil. 2. Then put haddock fillet inside and sprinkle it with cayenne pepper, salt, and heavy cream. Put the baking pan in the air fryer basket and cook at 192ºC for 8 minutes.

Black Cod with Grapes and Kale

Prep time: 10 minutes | Cook time: 15 minutes | Serves 2

2 (170 to 230 g) fillets of black cod
Salt and freshly ground black pepper, to taste
Olive oil
125 g grapes, halved
1 small bulb fennel, sliced
¼-inch thick
60 g pecans
60 g shredded kale
2 teaspoons white balsamic vinegar or white wine vinegar
2 tablespoons extra-virgin olive oil

1. Preheat the air fryer to 204ºC. 2. Season the cod fillets with salt and pepper and drizzle, brush or spray a little olive oil on top. Place the fish, presentation side up (skin side down), into the air fryer basket. Air fry for 10 minutes. 3. When the fish has finished cooking, remove the fillets to a side plate and loosely tent with foil to rest. 4. Toss the grapes, fennel and pecans in a bowl with a drizzle of olive oil and season with salt and pepper. Add the grapes, fennel and pecans to the air fryer basket and air fry for 5 minutes at 204ºC, shaking the basket once during the cooking time. 5. Transfer the grapes, fennel and pecans to a bowl with the kale. Dress the kale with the balsamic vinegar and olive oil, season to taste with salt and pepper and serve alongside the cooked fish.

Southern-Style Catfish

Prep time: 10 minutes | Cook time: 12 minutes | Serves 4

4 (200 g) catfish fillets
80 g heavy whipping cream
1 tablespoon lemon juice
125 g blanched finely ground almond flour
2 teaspoons Old Bay seasoning
½ teaspoon salt
¼ teaspoon ground black pepper

1. Place catfish fillets into a large bowl with cream and pour in lemon juice. Stir to coat. 2. In a separate large bowl, mix flour and Old Bay seasoning. 3. Remove each fillet and gently shake off excess cream. Sprinkle with salt and pepper. Press each fillet gently into flour mixture on both sides to coat. 4. Place fillets into ungreased air fryer basket. Adjust the temperature to 204ºC and air fry for 12 minutes, turning fillets halfway through cooking. Catfish will be golden brown and have an internal temperature of at least 64ºC when done. Serve warm.

Parmesan Lobster Tails

Prep time: 5 minutes | Cook time: 7 minutes | Serves 4

4 (110 g) lobster tails
2 tablespoons salted butter, melted
1½ teaspoons Cajun seasoning, divided
¼ teaspoon salt
¼ teaspoon ground black pepper
30 g grated Parmesan cheese
15 g plain pork scratchings, finely crushed

1. Cut lobster tails open carefully with a pair of scissors and gently pull meat away from shells, resting meat on top of shells. 2. Brush lobster meat with butter and sprinkle with 1 teaspoon Cajun seasoning, ¼ teaspoon per tail. 3. In a small bowl, mix remaining Cajun seasoning, salt, pepper, Parmesan, and pork scratchings. Gently press ¼ mixture onto meat on each lobster tail. 4. Carefully place tails into ungreased air fryer basket. Adjust the temperature to 204ºC and air fry for 7 minutes. Lobster tails will be crispy and golden on top and have an internal temperature of at least 64ºC when done. Serve warm.

Sweet Tilapia Fillets

Prep time: 5 minutes | Cook time: 14 minutes | Serves 4

2 tablespoons granulated sweetener
1 tablespoon apple cider vinegar
4 tilapia fillets, boneless
1 teaspoon olive oil

1. Mix apple cider vinegar with olive oil and sweetener. 2. Then rub the tilapia fillets with the sweet mixture and put in the air fryer basket in one layer. Cook the fish at 184ºC for 7 minutes per side.

Cayenne Flounder Cutlets

Prep time: 15 minutes | Cook time: 10 minutes | Serves 2

1 egg
125 g Pecorino Romano cheese, grated
Sea salt and white pepper, to taste
½ teaspoon cayenne pepper
1 teaspoon dried parsley flakes
2 flounder fillets

1. To make a breading station, whisk the egg until frothy. 2. In another bowl, mix Pecorino Romano cheese, and spices. 3. Dip the fish in the egg mixture and turn to coat evenly; then, dredge in the cracker crumb mixture, turning a couple of times to coat evenly. 4. Cook in the preheated air fryer at 200°C for 5 minutes; turn them over and cook another 5 minutes. Enjoy!

Savory Prawns

Prep time: 5 minutes | Cook time: 8 to 10 minutes | Serves 4

455 g fresh large prawns, peeled and deveined
1 tablespoon avocado oil
2 teaspoons minced garlic, divided
½ teaspoon red pepper flakes
Sea salt and freshly ground black pepper, to taste
2 tablespoons unsalted butter, melted
2 tablespoons chopped fresh parsley

1. Place the prawns in a large bowl and toss with the avocado oil, 1 teaspoon of minced garlic, and red pepper flakes. Season with salt and pepper. 2. Set the air fryer to 176°C. Arrange the prawns in a single layer in the air fryer basket, working in batches if necessary. Cook for 6 minutes. Flip the prawns and cook for 2 to 4 minutes more, until the internal temperature of the prawns reaches 48°C. (The time it takes to cook will depend on the size of the prawns). 3. While the prawns are cooking, melt the butter in a small saucepan over medium heat and stir in the remaining 1 teaspoon of garlic. 4. Transfer the cooked prawns to a large bowl, add the garlic butter, and toss well. Top with the parsley and serve warm.

Scallops in Lemon-Butter Sauce

Prep time: 10 minutes | Cook time: 6 minutes | Serves 2

8 large dry sea scallops (about 340 g)
Salt and freshly ground black pepper, to taste
2 tablespoons olive oil
2 tablespoons unsalted butter, melted
2 tablespoons chopped flat-leaf parsley
1 tablespoon fresh lemon juice
2 teaspoons capers, drained and chopped
1 teaspoon grated lemon zest
1 clove garlic, minced

1. Preheat the air fryer to 204°C. 2. Use a paper towel to pat the scallops dry. Sprinkle lightly with salt and pepper. Brush with the olive oil. Arrange the scallops in a single layer in the air fryer basket. Pausing halfway through the cooking time to turn the scallops, air fry for about 6 minutes until firm and opaque. 3. Meanwhile, in a small bowl, combine the oil, butter, parsley, lemon juice, capers, lemon zest, and garlic. Drizzle over the scallops just before serving.

Smoky Prawn and Chorizo Tapas

Prep time: 15 minutes | Cook time: 10 minutes | Serves 2 to 4

110 g Spanish (cured) chorizo, halved horizontally and sliced crosswise
230 g raw medium prawns, peeled and deveined
1 tablespoon extra-virgin olive oil
1 small shallot, halved and thinly sliced
1 garlic clove, minced
1 tablespoon finely chopped fresh oregano
½ teaspoon smoked Spanish paprika
¼ teaspoon kosher or coarse sea salt
¼ teaspoon black pepper
3 tablespoons fresh orange juice
1 tablespoon minced fresh parsley

1. Place the chorizo in a baking pan. Set the pan in the air fryer basket. Set the air fryer to 192°C for 5 minutes, or until the chorizo has started to brown and render its fat. 2. Meanwhile, in a large bowl, combine the prawns, olive oil, shallot, garlic, oregano, paprika, salt, and pepper. Toss until the prawns are well coated. 3. Transfer the prawns to the pan with the chorizo. Stir to combine. Place the pan in the air fryer basket. Cook for 10 minutes, stirring halfway through the cooking time. 4. Transfer the prawns and chorizo to a serving dish. Drizzle with the orange juice and toss to combine. Sprinkle with the parsley.

Oregano Tilapia Fingers

Prep time: 15 minutes | Cook time: 9 minutes | Serves 4

455 g tilapia fillet
60 g coconut flour
2 eggs, beaten
½ teaspoon ground paprika
1 teaspoon dried oregano
1 teaspoon avocado oil

1. Cut the tilapia fillets into fingers and sprinkle with ground paprika and dried oregano. 2. Then dip the tilapia fingers in eggs and coat in the coconut flour. 3. Sprinkle fish fingers with avocado oil and cook in the air fryer at 188°C for 9 minutes.

Almond-Crusted Fish

Prep time: 15 minutes | Cook time: 10 minutes | Serves 4

4 (110 g) fish fillets
95 g bread crumbs
30 g sliced almonds, crushed
2 tablespoons lemon juice
⅛ teaspoon cayenne
Salt and pepper, to taste
95 g flour
1 egg, beaten with 1 tablespoon water
Oil for misting or cooking spray

1. Split fish fillets lengthwise down the center to create 8 pieces. 2. Mix bread crumbs and almonds together and set aside. 3. Mix the lemon juice and cayenne together. Brush on all sides of fish. 4. Season fish to taste with salt and pepper. 5. Place the flour on a sheet of wax paper. 6. Roll fillets in flour, dip in egg wash, and roll in the crumb mixture. 7. Mist both sides of fish with oil or cooking spray. 8. Spray the air fryer basket and lay fillets inside. 9. Roast at 200°C for 5 minutes, turn fish over, and cook for an additional 5 minutes or until fish is done and flakes easily.

Roasted Fish with Almond-Lemon Crumbs

Prep time: 10 minutes | Cook time: 7 to 8 minutes | Serves 4

60 g raw whole almonds
1 scallion, finely chopped
Grated zest and juice of 1 lemon
½ tablespoon extra-virgin olive oil
¾ teaspoon kosher or coarse sea salt, divided
Freshly ground black pepper, to taste
2 spring onions, chopped
4 (170 g) skinless fish fillets
Cooking spray
1 teaspoon Dijon mustard

1. In a food processor, pulse the almonds to coarsely chop. Transfer to a small bowl and add the spring onions, lemon zest, and olive oil. Season with ¼ teaspoon of the salt and pepper to taste and mix to combine. 2. Spray the top of the fish with oil and squeeze the lemon juice over the fish. Season with the remaining ½ teaspoon salt and pepper to taste. Spread the mustard on top of the fish. Dividing evenly, press the almond mixture onto the top of the fillets to adhere. 3. Preheat the air fryer to 192°C. 4. Working in batches, place the fillets in the air fryer basket in a single layer. Air fry for 7 to 8 minutes, until the crumbs start to brown and the fish is cooked through. 5. Serve immediately.

Tilapia Sandwiches with Tartar Sauce

Prep time: 8 minutes | Cook time: 17 minutes | Serves 4

185 g mayonnaise
2 tablespoons dried minced onion
1 dill pickle spear, finely chopped
2 teaspoons pickle juice
¼ teaspoon salt
⅛ teaspoon freshly ground black pepper
40 g plain flour
1 egg, lightly beaten
220 g panko bread crumbs
2 teaspoons lemon pepper
4 (170 g) tilapia fillets
Olive oil spray
4 soft subway rolls
4 butter lettuce leaves

1. To make the tartar sauce, in a small bowl, whisk the mayonnaise, dried onion, pickle, pickle juice, salt, and pepper until blended. Refrigerate while you make the fish. 2. Scoop the flour onto a plate; set aside. 3. Put the beaten egg in a medium shallow bowl. 4. On another plate, stir together the panko and lemon pepper. 5. Insert the crisper plate into the basket and the basket into the unit. Preheat the unit by selecting AIR FRY, setting the temperature to 204°C, and setting the time to 3 minutes. Select START/STOP to begin. 6. Dredge the tilapia fillets in the flour, in the egg, and press into the panko mixture to coat. 7. Once the unit is preheated, spray the crisper plate with olive oil and place a baking paper liner into the basket. Place the prepared fillets on the liner in a single layer. Lightly spray the fillets with olive oil. 8. Select AIR FRY, set the temperature to 204°C, and set the time to 17 minutes. Select START/STOP to begin. 9. After 8 minutes, remove the basket, carefully flip the fillets, and spray them with more olive oil. Reinsert the basket to resume cooking. 10. When the cooking is complete, the fillets should be golden and crispy and a food thermometer should register 64°C. Place each cooked fillet in a subway roll, top with a little bit of tartar sauce and lettuce, and serve.

Mustard-Crusted Fish Fillets

Prep time: 5 minutes | Cook time: 8 to 11 minutes | Serves 4

5 teaspoons low-sodium yellow mustard
1 tablespoon freshly squeezed lemon juice
4 (100 g) sole fillets
½ teaspoon dried thyme
½ teaspoon dried marjoram
⅛ teaspoon freshly ground black pepper
1 slice low-sodium whole-wheat bread, crumbled
2 teaspoons olive oil

1. In a small bowl, mix the mustard and lemon juice. Spread this evenly over the fillets. Place them in the air fryer basket. 2. In another small bowl, mix the thyme, marjoram, pepper, bread crumbs, and olive oil. Mix until combined. 3. Gently but firmly press the spice mixture onto the top of each fish fillet. 4. Bake at 160°C for 8 to 11 minutes, or until the fish reaches an internal temperature of at least 64°C on a meat thermometer and the topping is browned and crisp. Serve immediately.

Marinated Salmon Fillets

Prep time: 10 minutes | Cook time: 15 to 20 minutes | Serves 4

60 g soy sauce
65 ml rice wine vinegar
1 tablespoon brown sugar
1 tablespoon olive oil
1 teaspoon mustard powder
1 teaspoon ground ginger
½ teaspoon freshly ground black pepper
½ teaspoon minced garlic
4 (170 g) salmon fillets, skin-on
Cooking spray

1. In a small bowl, combine the soy sauce, rice wine vinegar, brown sugar, olive oil, mustard powder, ginger, black pepper, and garlic to make a marinade. 2. Place the fillets in a shallow baking dish and pour the marinade over them. Cover the baking dish and marinate for at least 1 hour in the refrigerator, turning the fillets occasionally to keep them coated in the marinade. 3. Preheat the air fryer to 188°C. Spray the air fryer basket lightly with cooking spray. 4. Shake off as much marinade as possible from the fillets and place them, skin-side down, in the air fryer basket in a single layer. You may need to cook the fillets in batches. 5. Air fry for 15 to 20 minutes for well done. The minimum internal temperature should be 64°C at the thickest part of the fillets. 6. Serve hot.

Almond Catfish

Prep time: 10 minutes | Cook time: 12 minutes | Serves 4

910 g catfish fillet
60 g almond flour
2 eggs, beaten
1 teaspoon salt
1 teaspoon avocado oil

1. Sprinkle the catfish fillet with salt and dip in the eggs. 2. Then coat the fish in the almond flour and put in the air fryer basket. Sprinkle the fish with avocado oil. 3. Cook the fish for 6 minutes per side at 192°C.

Chapter 6 Beef, Pork, and Lamb

Garlic Balsamic Beef

Prep time: 30 minutes | Cook time: 8 to 10 minutes | Serves 8

910 g topside beef
3 large garlic cloves, minced
3 tablespoons balsamic vinegar
3 tablespoons whole grain mustard
2 tablespoons olive oil
Sea salt and ground black pepper, to taste
½ teaspoon dried hot red pepper flakes

1. Score both sides of the cleaned beef. 2. Thoroughly combine the remaining ingredients; massage this mixture into the meat to coat it on all sides. Let it marinate for at least 3 hours. 3. Set the air fryer to 204°C; then cook the beef for 15 minutes. Flip it over and cook another 10 to 12 minutes. Bon appétit!

Beef Burger

Prep time: 20 minutes | Cook time: 12 minutes | Serves 4

570 g lean minced beef
1 tablespoon coconut aminos or tamari
1 teaspoon Dijon mustard
A few dashes of liquid smoke
1 teaspoon shallot powder
1 clove garlic, minced
½ teaspoon cumin powder
30 g spring onions, minced
⅓ teaspoon sea salt flakes
⅓ teaspoon freshly cracked mixed peppercorns
1 teaspoon celery seeds
1 teaspoon parsley flakes

1. Mix all of the above ingredients in a bowl; knead until everything is well incorporated. 2. Shape the mixture into four patties. Next, make a shallow dip in the center of each patty to prevent them puffing up during air frying. 3. Spritz the patties on all sides using nonstick cooking spray. Cook approximately 12 minutes at 184°C. 4. Check for doneness, an instant-read thermometer should read 72°C. Bon appétit!

Bacon, Cheese and Pear Stuffed Pork

Prep time: 10 minutes | Cook time: 24 minutes | Serves 3

4 slices bacon, chopped
1 tablespoon butter
60 g finely diced onion
80 ml chicken stock
185 g seasoned stuffing cubes
1 egg, beaten
½ teaspoon dried thyme
½ teaspoon salt
⅛ teaspoon black pepper
1 pear, finely diced
40 g crumbled blue cheese
3 boneless center-cut pork chops (2-inch thick)
Olive oil
Salt and freshly ground black pepper, to taste

1. Preheat the air fryer to 204°C. 2. Place the bacon into the air fryer basket and air fry for 6 minutes, stirring halfway through the cooking time. Remove the bacon and set it aside on a paper towel. Pour out the grease from the bottom of the air fryer. 3. Make the stuffing: Melt the butter in a medium saucepan over medium heat on the stovetop. Add the onion and sauté for a few minutes, until it starts to soften. Add the chicken stock and simmer for 1 minute. Remove the pan from the heat and add the stuffing cubes. Stir until the stock has been absorbed. Add the egg, dried thyme, salt and freshly ground black pepper, and stir until combined. Fold in the diced pear and crumbled blue cheese. 4. Place the pork chops on a cutting board. Using the palm of your hand to hold the chop flat and steady, slice into the side of the pork chop to make a pocket in the center of the chop. Leave about an inch of chop uncut and make sure you don't cut all the way through the pork chop. Brush both sides of the pork chops with olive oil and season with salt and freshly ground black pepper. Stuff each pork chop with a third of the stuffing, packing the stuffing tightly inside the pocket. 5. Preheat the air fryer to 184°C. 6. Spray or brush the sides of the air fryer basket with oil. Place the pork chops in the air fryer basket with the open stuffed edge of the pork chop facing the outside edges of the basket. 7. Air fry the pork chops for 18 minutes, turning the pork chops over halfway through the cooking time. When the chops are done, let them rest for 5 minutes and then transfer to a serving platter.

Greek Stuffed Tenderloin

Prep time: 10 minutes | Cook time: 10 minutes | Serves 4

680 g venison or beef tenderloin, pounded to ¼ inch thick
3 teaspoons fine sea salt
1 teaspoon ground black pepper
60 g creamy goat cheese
60 g crumbled feta cheese
30 g finely chopped onions
2 cloves garlic, minced
For Garnish/Serving (Optional):
Prepared yellow mustard
Halved cherry tomatoes
Extra-virgin olive oil
Sprigs of fresh rosemary
Lavender flowers

1. Spray the air fryer basket with avocado oil. Preheat the air fryer to 204°C. 2. Season the tenderloin on all sides with the salt and pepper. 3. In a medium-sized mixing bowl, combine the goat cheese, feta, onions, and garlic. Place the mixture in the center of the tenderloin. Starting at the end closest to you, tightly roll the tenderloin like a jelly roll. Tie the rolled tenderloin tightly with kitchen twine. 4. Place the meat in the air fryer basket and air fry for 5 minutes. Flip the meat over and cook for another 5 minutes, or until the internal temperature reaches 56°C for medium-rare. 5. To serve, smear a line of prepared yellow mustard on a platter, then place the meat next to it and add halved cherry tomatoes on the side, if desired. Drizzle with olive oil and garnish with rosemary sprigs and lavender flowers, if desired. 6. Best served fresh. Store leftovers in an airtight container in the fridge for 3 days. Reheat in a preheated 176°C air fryer for 4 minutes, or until heated through.

Smothered Chops

Prep time: 20 minutes | Cook time: 30 minutes | Serves 4

4 bone-in pork chops (230 g each)
2 teaspoons salt, divided
1½ teaspoons freshly ground black pepper, divided
1 teaspoon garlic powder
250 g tomato purée
1½ teaspoons Italian seasoning
1 tablespoon sugar
1 tablespoon cornflour
60 g chopped onion
60 g chopped green bell pepper
1 to 2 tablespoons oil

1. Evenly season the pork chops with 1 teaspoon salt, 1 teaspoon pepper, and the garlic powder. 2. In a medium bowl, stir together the tomato purée, Italian seasoning, sugar, remaining 1 teaspoon of salt, and remaining ½ teaspoon of pepper. 3. In a small bowl, whisk 185 ml water and the cornflour until blended. Stir this slurry into the tomato purée, with the onion and green bell pepper. Transfer to a baking pan. 4. Preheat the air fryer to 176ºC. 5. Place the sauce in the fryer and cook for 10 minutes. Stir and cook for 10 minutes more. Remove the pan and keep warm. 6. Increase the air fryer temperature to 204ºC. Line the air fryer basket with baking paper. 7. Place the pork chops on the baking paper and spritz with oil. 8. Cook for 5 minutes. Flip and spritz the chops with oil and cook for 5 minutes more, until the internal temperature reaches 64ºC. Serve with the tomato mixture spooned on top.

Pork Medallions with Radicchio and Endive Salad

Prep time: 25 minutes | Cook time: 7 minutes | Serves 4

1 (230 g) pork tenderloin
Salt and freshly ground black pepper, to taste
30 g plain flour
2 eggs, lightly beaten
95 g matzo meal
1 teaspoon paprika
1 teaspoon dry mustard
1 teaspoon garlic powder
1 teaspoon dried thyme
1 teaspoon salt
Vegetable or canola oil, in spray bottle
Vinaigrette:
65 ml white balsamic vinegar
2 tablespoons agave syrup (or honey or maple syrup)
1 tablespoon Dijon mustard
Juice of ½ lemon
2 tablespoons chopped chervil or flat-leaf parsley
Salt and freshly ground black pepper
125 ml extra-virgin olive oil
Radicchio and Endive Salad:
1 heart romaine lettuce, torn into large pieces
½ head radicchio, coarsely chopped
2 heads endive, sliced
60 g cherry tomatoes, halved
85 g fresh Mozzarella, diced
Salt and freshly ground black pepper, to taste

1. Slice the pork tenderloin into 1-inch slices. Using a meat pounder, pound the pork slices into thin ½-inch medallions. Generously season the pork with salt and freshly ground black pepper on both sides. 2. Set up a dredging station using three shallow dishes. Put the flour in one dish and the beaten eggs in a second dish. Combine the matzo meal, paprika, dry mustard, garlic powder, thyme and salt in a third dish. 3. Preheat the air fryer to 204ºC. 4. Dredge the pork medallions in flour first and then into the beaten egg. Let the excess egg drip off and coat both sides of the medallions with the matzo meal crumb mixture. Spray both sides of the coated medallions with vegetable or canola oil. 5. Air fry the medallions in two batches at 204ºC for 5 minutes. Once you have air-fried all the medallions, flip them all over and return the first batch of medallions back into the air fryer on top of the second batch. Air fry at 204ºC for an additional 2 minutes. 6. While the medallions are cooking, make the salad and dressing. Whisk the white balsamic vinegar, agave syrup, Dijon mustard, lemon juice, chervil, salt and pepper together in a small bowl. Whisk in the olive oil slowly until combined and thickened. 7. Combine the romaine lettuce, radicchio, endive, cherry tomatoes, and Mozzarella cheese in a large salad bowl. Drizzle the dressing over the vegetables and toss to combine. Season with salt and freshly ground black pepper. 8. Serve the pork medallions warm on or beside the salad.

Korean Beef Tacos

Prep time: 30 minutes | Cook time: 12 minutes | Serves 6

2 tablespoons gochujang (Korean red chilli paste)
2 cloves garlic, minced
2 teaspoons minced fresh ginger
2 tablespoons toasted sesame oil
1 tablespoon soy sauce
2 tablespoons sesame seeds
2 teaspoons sugar
½ teaspoon kosher or coarse sea salt
680 g thinly sliced beef (chuck, rib eye, or sirloin)
1 medium red onion, sliced
12 (6-inch) flour tortillas, warmed; or lettuce leaves
60 g chopped green onions
5 g chopped fresh coriander (optional)
60 g kimchi (optional)

1. In a small bowl, combine the gochujang, garlic, ginger, sesame oil, soy sauce, sesame seeds, sugar, and salt. Whisk until well combined. Place the beef and red onion in a large sandwich bag and pour the marinade over. Seal the bag and massage to coat all of the meat and onion. Marinate at room temperature for 30 minutes or in the refrigerator for up to 24 hours. 2. Place the meat and onion in the air fryer basket, leaving behind as much of the marinade as possible; discard the marinade. Set the air fryer to 204ºC for 12 minutes, shaking halfway through the cooking time. 3. To serve, place meat and onion in the tortillas. Top with the green onions and the coriander and kimchi, if using, and serve.

Peppercorn-Crusted Beef Tenderloin

Prep time: 10 minutes | Cook time: 25 minutes | Serves 6

2 tablespoons salted butter, melted
2 teaspoons minced roasted garlic
3 tablespoons ground 4-peppercorn blend
1 (910 g) beef tenderloin, trimmed of visible fat

1. In a small bowl, mix the butter and roasted garlic. Brush it over the beef tenderloin. 2. Place the ground peppercorns onto a plate and roll the tenderloin through them, creating a crust. Place tenderloin into the air fryer basket. 3. Adjust the temperature to 204ºC and roast for 25 minutes. 4. Turn the tenderloin halfway through the cooking time. 5. Allow meat to rest 10 minutes before slicing.

Pork Schnitzels with Sour Cream and Dill Sauce

Prep time: 5 minutes | Cook time: 24 minutes | Serves 4 to 6

60 g plain flour
1½ teaspoons salt
Freshly ground black pepper, to taste
2 eggs
125 ml milk
185 g toasted breadcrumbs
1 teaspoon paprika
6 boneless, center cut pork chops (about 680 g), fat trimmed, pound to ½-inch thick
2 tablespoons olive oil
3 tablespoons melted butter
Lemon wedges, for serving
Sour Cream and Dill Sauce:
250 ml chicken stock
1½ tablespoons cornflour
80 ml sour cream
1½ tablespoons chopped fresh dill
Salt and ground black pepper, to taste

1. Preheat the air fryer to 204ºC. 2. Combine the flour with salt and black pepper in a large bowl. Stir to mix well. Whisk the egg with milk in a second bowl. Stir the breadcrumbs and paprika in a third bowl. 3. Dredge the pork chops in the flour bowl, then in the egg milk, and then into the breadcrumbs bowl. Press to coat well. Shake the excess off. 4. Arrange one pork chop in the preheated air fryer each time, then brush with olive oil and butter on all sides. 5. Air fry each pork chop for 4 minutes or until golden brown and crispy. Flip the chop halfway through the cooking time. 6. Transfer the cooked pork chop (schnitzel) to a baking pan in the oven and keep warm over low heat while air frying the remaining pork chops. 7. Meanwhile, combine the chicken stock and cornflour in a small saucepan and bring to a boil over medium-high heat. Simmer for 2 more minutes. 8. Turn off the heat, then mix in the sour cream, fresh dill, salt, and black pepper. 9. Remove the schnitzels from the air fryer to a plate and baste with sour cream and dill sauce. Squeeze the lemon wedges over and slice to serve.

Spicy Flank Steak with Zhoug

Prep time: 30 minutes | Cook time: 8 minutes | Serves 4

Marinade and Steak:
125 ml dark beer or orange juice
65 ml fresh lemon juice
3 cloves garlic, minced
2 tablespoons extra-virgin olive oil
2 tablespoons Sriracha
2 tablespoons brown sugar
2 teaspoons ground cumin
2 teaspoons smoked paprika
1 tablespoon kosher or coarse sea salt
1 teaspoon black pepper
680 g flank steak, trimmed and cut into 3 pieces
Zhoug:
20 g packed fresh coriander leaves
2 cloves garlic, peeled
2 jalapeño or serrano chillies, stemmed and coarsely chopped
½ teaspoon ground cumin
¼ teaspoon ground coriander
¼ teaspoon kosher or coarse sea salt
2 to 4 tablespoons extra-virgin olive oil

1. For the marinade and steak: In a small bowl, whisk together the beer, lemon juice, garlic, olive oil, Sriracha, brown sugar, cumin, paprika, salt, and pepper. Place the steak in a large sandwich bag. Pour the marinade over the steak, seal the bag, and massage the steak to coat. Marinate in the refrigerator for 1 hour or up to 24 hours, turning the bag occasionally. 2. Meanwhile, for the Zhoug: In a food processor, combine the coriander, garlic, jalapeños, cumin, coriander, and salt. Process until finely chopped. Add 2 tablespoons olive oil and pulse to form a loose paste, adding up to 2 tablespoons more olive oil if needed. Transfer the Zhoug to a glass container. Cover and store in the refrigerator until 30 minutes before serving if marinating more than 1 hour. 3. Remove the steak from the marinade and discard the marinade. Place the steak in the air fryer basket and set the air fryer to 204ºC for 8 minutes. Use a meat thermometer to ensure the steak has reached an internal temperature of 64ºC (for medium). 4. Transfer the steak to a cutting board and let rest for 5 minutes. Slice the steak across the grain and serve with the Zhoug.

Roast Beef with Horseradish Cream

Prep time: 5 minutes | Cook time: 35 to 45 minutes | Serves 6

910 g beef roast top round or eye of round
1 tablespoon salt
2 teaspoons garlic powder
1 teaspoon freshly ground black pepper
1 teaspoon dried thyme
Horseradish Cream:
80 g heavy cream
80 g sour cream
80 g prepared horseradish
2 teaspoons fresh lemon juice
Salt and freshly ground black pepper, to taste

1. Preheat the air fryer to 204ºC. 2. Season the beef with the salt, garlic powder, black pepper, and thyme. Place the beef fat-side down in the basket of the air fryer and lightly coat with olive oil. Pausing halfway through the cooking time to turn the meat, air fry for 35 to 45 minutes, until a thermometer inserted into the thickest part indicates the desired doneness, 52ºC (rare) to 64ºC (medium). Let the beef rest for 10 minutes before slicing. 3. To make the horseradish cream: In a small bowl, combine the heavy cream, sour cream, horseradish, and lemon juice. Whisk until thoroughly combined. Season to taste with salt and freshly ground black pepper. Serve alongside the beef.

Blackened Cajun Pork Roast

Prep time: 20 minutes | Cook time: 33 minutes | Serves 4

910 g bone-in pork loin roast
2 tablespoons oil
30 g Cajun seasoning
60 g diced onion
10 g diced celery
60 g diced green bell pepper
1 tablespoon minced garlic

1. Cut 5 slits across the pork roast. Spritz it with oil, coating it completely. Evenly sprinkle the Cajun seasoning over the pork roast. 2. In a medium bowl, stir together the onion, celery, green bell pepper, and garlic until combined. Set aside. 3. Preheat the air fryer to 184ºC. Line the air fryer basket with baking paper. 4. Place the pork roast on the baking paper and spritz with oil. 5. Cook for 5 minutes. Flip the roast and cook for 5 minutes more. Continue to flip and cook in 5-minute increments for a total cook time of 20 minutes. 6. Increase the air fryer temperature to 200ºC. 7. Cook the roast for 8 minutes more and flip. Add the vegetable mixture to the basket and cook for a final 5 minutes. Let the roast sit for 5 minutes before serving.

Kielbasa Sausage with Pineapple and Bell Peppers

Prep time: 15 minutes | Cook time: 10 minutes | Serves 2 to 4

340 g kielbasa sausage, cut into ½-inch slices
1 (230 g) can pineapple chunks in juice, drained
125 g bell pepper chunks
1 tablespoon barbecue seasoning
1 tablespoon soy sauce
Cooking spray

1. Preheat the air fryer to 200°C. Spritz the air fryer basket with cooking spray. 2. Combine all the ingredients in a large bowl. Toss to mix well. 3. Pour the sausage mixture in the preheated air fryer. 4. Air fry for 10 minutes or until the sausage is lightly browned and the bell pepper and pineapple are soft. Shake the basket halfway through. Serve immediately.

Beef Flank Steak with Sage

Prep time: 13 minutes | Cook time: 7 minutes | Serves 2

80 g sour cream
60 g spring onion, chopped
1 tablespoon mayonnaise
3 cloves garlic, smashed
455 g beef flank steak, trimmed and cubed
2 tablespoons fresh sage, minced
½ teaspoon salt
⅓ teaspoon black pepper, or to taste

1. Season your meat with salt and pepper; arrange beef cubes on the bottom of a baking dish that fits in your air fryer. 2. Stir in spring onions and garlic; air fry for about 7 minutes at 196°C. 3. Once your beef starts to tender, add the cream, mayonnaise, and sage; air fry an additional 8 minutes. Bon appétit!

Pork and Pinto Bean Gorditas

Prep time: 20 minutes | Cook time: 21 minutes | Serves 4

455 g lean minced pork
2 tablespoons chilli powder
2 tablespoons ground cumin
1 teaspoon dried oregano
2 teaspoons paprika
1 teaspoon garlic powder
125 ml water
1 (425 g) can pinto beans, drained and rinsed
125 g taco sauce
Salt and freshly ground black pepper, to taste
250 g grated Cheddar cheese
5 (12-inch) flour tortillas
4 (8-inch) crispy corn tortilla shells
80 g shredded lettuce
1 tomato, diced
40 g sliced black olives
Sour cream, for serving
Tomato salsa, for serving
Cooking spray

1. Preheat the air fryer to 204°C. Spritz the air fryer basket with cooking spray. 2. Put the minced pork in the air fryer basket and air fry at 204°C for 10 minutes, stirring a few times to gently break up the meat. Combine the chilli powder, cumin, oregano, paprika, garlic powder and water in a small bowl. Stir the spice mixture into the browned pork. Stir in the beans and taco sauce and air fry for an additional minute. Transfer the pork mixture to a bowl. Season with salt and freshly ground black pepper. 3. Sprinkle 60 g the grated cheese in the center of the flour tortillas, leaving a 2-inch border around the edge free of cheese and filling. Divide the pork mixture among the four tortillas, placing it on top of the cheese. Put a crunchy corn tortilla on top of the pork and top with shredded lettuce, diced tomatoes, and black olives. Cut the remaining flour tortilla into 4 quarters. These quarters of tortilla will serve as the bottom of the gorditPut one quarter tortilla on top of each gordita and fold the edges of the bottom flour tortilla up over the sides, enclosing the filling. While holding the seams down, brush the bottom of the gordita with olive oil and place the seam side down on the countertop while you finish the remaining three gorditas. 4. Adjust the temperature to 192°C. 5. Air fry one gordita at a time. Transfer the gordita carefully to the air fryer basket, seam side down. Brush or spray the top tortilla with oil and air fry for 5 minutes. Carefully turn the gordita over and air fry for an additional 4 to 5 minutes until both sides are browned. When finished air frying all four gorditas, layer them back into the air fryer for an additional minute to make sure they are all warm before serving with sour cream and salsa.

Air Fryer Chicken-Fried Steak

Prep time: 5 minutes | Cook time: 20 minutes | Serves 4

455 g beef sirloin steak
750 ml skimmed milk, divided
1 teaspoon dried thyme
1 teaspoon dried rosemary
2 medium egg whites
125 g chickpea crumbs
60 g coconut flour
1 tablespoon Creole seasoning

1. In a bowl, marinate the steak in 500 ml milk for 30 to 45 minutes. 2. Remove the steak from milk, shake off the excess liquid, and season with the thyme and rosemary. Discard the milk. 3. In a shallow bowl, beat the egg whites with the remaining 250 ml milk. 4. In a separate shallow bowl, combine the chickpea crumbs, coconut flour, and seasoning. 5. Dip the steak in the egg white mixture then dredge in the chickpea crumb mixture, coating well. 6. Place the steak in the basket of an air fryer. 7. Set the air fryer to 390°F, close, and cook for 10 minutes. 8. Open the air fryer, turn the steaks, close, and cook for 10 minutes. Let rest for 5 minutes.

Herb-Roasted Beef Tips with Onions

Prep time: 5 minutes | Cook time: 10 minutes | Serves 4

455 g rib eye steak, cubed
2 garlic cloves, minced
2 tablespoons olive oil
1 tablespoon fresh oregano
1 teaspoon salt
½ teaspoon black pepper
1 yellow onion, thinly sliced

1. Preheat the air fryer to 192°C. 2. In a medium bowl, combine the steak, garlic, olive oil, oregano, salt, pepper, and onion. Mix until all of the beef and onion are well coated. 3. Put the seasoned steak mixture into the air fryer basket. Roast for 5 minutes. Stir and roast for 5 minutes more. 4. Let rest for 5 minutes before serving with some favorite sides.

Bacon-Wrapped Cheese Pork

Prep time: 10 minutes | Cook time: 20 minutes | Serves 4

4 (1-inch-thick) boneless pork chops
2 (150 g) packages Boursin cheese
8 slices thin-cut bacon
Avocado oil for spraying

1. Spray the air fryer basket with avocado oil. Preheat the air fryer to 204ºC. 2. Place one of the chops on a cutting board. With a sharp knife held parallel to the cutting board, make a 1-inch-wide incision on the top edge of the chop. Carefully cut into the chop to form a large pocket, leaving a ½-inch border along the sides and bottom. Repeat with the other 3 chops. 3. Snip the corner of a large resealable sandwich bag to form a ¾-inch hole. Place the Boursin cheese in the bag and pipe the cheese into the pockets in the chops, dividing the cheese evenly among them. 4. Wrap 2 slices of bacon around each chop and secure the ends with toothpicks. Place the bacon-wrapped chops in the air fryer basket and cook for 10 minutes, then flip the chops and cook for another 8 to 10 minutes, until the bacon is crisp, the chops are cooked through, and the internal temperature reaches 64ºC. 5. Store leftovers in an airtight container in the refrigerator for up to 3 days. Reheat in a preheated 204ºC air fryer for 5 minutes, or until warmed through.

Pork Tenderloin with Avocado Lime Sauce

Prep time: 30 minutes | Cook time: 15 minutes | Serves 4

Marinade:
125 ml lime juice
Grated zest of 1 lime
2 teaspoons granulated sweetener, or ¼ teaspoon liquid sweetener
3 cloves garlic, minced
1½ teaspoons fine sea salt
1 teaspoon chilli powder, or more for more heat
1 teaspoon smoked paprika
455 g pork tenderloin
Avocado Lime Sauce:
1 medium-sized ripe avocado, roughly chopped
125 g full-fat sour cream (or coconut cream for dairy-free)
Grated zest of 1 lime
Juice of 1 lime
2 cloves garlic, roughly chopped
½ teaspoon fine sea salt
¼ teaspoon ground black pepper
Chopped fresh coriander leaves, for garnish
Lime slices, for serving
Pico de Gallo, for serving

1. In a medium-sized casserole dish, stir together all the marinade ingredients until well combined. Add the tenderloin and coat it well in the marinade. Cover and place in the fridge to marinate for 2 hours or overnight. 2. Spray the air fryer basket with avocado oil. Preheat the air fryer to 204ºC. 3. Remove the pork from the marinade and place it in the air fryer basket. Air fry for 13 to 15 minutes, until the internal temperature of the pork is 64ºC, flipping after 7 minutes. Remove the pork from the air fryer and place it on a cutting board. Allow it to rest for 8 to 10 minutes, then cut it into ½-inch-thick slices. 4. While the pork cooks, make the avocado lime sauce: Place all the sauce ingredients in a food processor and purée until smooth. Taste and adjust the seasoning to your liking. 5. Place the pork slices on a serving platter and spoon the avocado lime sauce on top. Garnish with coriander leaves and serve with lime slices and Pico de Gallo. 6. Store leftovers in an airtight container in the fridge for up to 4 days. Reheat in a preheated 204ºC air fryer for 5 minutes, or until heated through.

Pork Schnitzel with Dill Sauce

Prep time: 5 minutes | Cook time: 24 minutes | Serves 4 to 6

6 boneless, center cut pork chops (about 680 g)
60 g plain flour
1½ teaspoons salt
Freshly ground black pepper, to taste
2 eggs
125 ml milk
185 g toasted fine bread crumbs
1 teaspoon paprika
3 tablespoons butter, melted
2 tablespoons vegetable or olive oil
Lemon wedges
Dill Sauce:
250 ml chicken stock
1½ tablespoons cornflour
80 g sour cream
1½ tablespoons chopped fresh dill
Salt and pepper, to taste

1.Trim the excess fat from the pork chops and pound each chop with a meat mallet between two pieces of plastic wrap until they are ½-inch thick. 2. Set up a dredging station. Combine the flour, salt, and black pepper in a shallow dish. Whisk the eggs and milk together in a second shallow dish. Finally, combine the bread crumbs and paprika in a third shallow dish. 3. Dip each flattened pork chop in the flour. Shake off the excess flour and dip each chop into the egg mixture. Finally dip them into the bread crumbs and press the bread crumbs onto the meat firmly. Place each finished chop on a baking sheet until they are all coated. 4. Preheat the air fryer to 204ºC. 5. Combine the melted butter and the oil in a small bowl and lightly brush both sides of the coated pork chops. Do not brush the chops too heavily or the breading will not be as crispy. 6. Air fry one schnitzel at a time for 4 minutes, turning it over halfway through the cooking time. Hold the cooked schnitzels warm on a baking pan in a 76ºC oven while you finish air frying the rest. 7. While the schnitzels are cooking, whisk the chicken stock and cornflour together in a small saucepan over medium-high heat on the stovetop. Bring the mixture to a boil and simmer for 2 minutes. Remove the saucepan from heat and whisk in the sour cream. Add the chopped fresh dill and season with salt and pepper. 8. Transfer the pork schnitzel to a platter and serve with dill sauce and lemon wedges.

Onion Pork Kebabs

Prep time: 22 minutes | Cook time: 18 minutes | Serves 3

2 tablespoons tomato purée
½ fresh Serrano chilli, minced
⅓ teaspoon paprika
455 g pork, ground
60 g spring onions, finely chopped
3 cloves garlic, peeled and finely minced
1 teaspoon ground black pepper, or more to taste
1 teaspoon salt, or more to taste

1. Thoroughly combine all ingredients in a mixing dish. Then form your mixture into sausage shapes. 2. Cook for 18 minutes at 180ºC. Mound salad on a serving platter, top with air-fried kebabs and serve warm. Bon appétit!

Cube Steak Roll-Ups

Prep time: 30 minutes | Cook time: 8 to 10 minutes | Serves 4

4 cube steaks (170 g each)
1 (455 g) bottle Italian dressing
1 teaspoon salt
½ teaspoon freshly ground black pepper
60 g finely chopped yellow onion
60 g finely chopped green bell pepper
60 g finely chopped mushrooms
1 to 2 tablespoons oil

1. In a large sandwich bag or airtight storage container, combine the steaks and Italian dressing. Seal the bag and refrigerate to marinate for 2 hours. 2. Remove the steaks from the marinade and place them on a cutting board. Discard the marinade. Evenly season the steaks with salt and pepper. 3. In a small bowl, stir together the onion, bell pepper, and mushrooms. Sprinkle the onion mixture evenly over the steaks. Roll up the steaks, Swiss roll-style, and secure with toothpicks. 4. Preheat the air fryer to 204°C. 5. Place the steaks in the air fryer basket. 6. Cook for 4 minutes. Flip the steaks and spritz them with oil. Cook for 4 to 6 minutes more until the internal temperature reaches 64°C. Let rest for 5 minutes before serving.

Chapter 7 Snacks and Appetisers

Cheesy Steak Fries

Prep time: 5 minutes | Cook time: 20 minutes | Serves 5

1 (800 g) bag frozen steak-cut fries
Cooking spray
Salt and pepper, to taste
125 g beef gravy
125 g shredded Mozzarella cheese
2 spring onions, green parts only, chopped

1. Preheat the air fryer to 204°C. 2. Place the frozen steak-cut fries in the air fryer. Air fry for 10 minutes. Shake the basket and spritz the fries with cooking spray. Sprinkle with salt and pepper. Air fry for an additional 8 minutes. 3. Pour the beef gravy into a medium, microwave-safe bowl. Microwave for 30 seconds, or until the gravy is warm. 4. Sprinkle the fries with the cheese. Air fry for an additional 2 minutes, until the cheese is melted. 5. Transfer the fries to a serving dish. Drizzle the fries with gravy and sprinkle the spring onions on top for a green garnish. Serve.

Crispy Chilli Chickpeas

Prep time: 5 minutes | Cook time: 15 minutes | Serves 4

1 (425 g) can cooked chickpeas, drained and rinsed
1 tablespoon olive oil
¼ teaspoon salt
⅛ teaspoon chilli powder
⅛ teaspoon garlic powder
⅛ teaspoon paprika

1. Preheat the air fryer to 192°C. 2. In a medium bowl, toss all of the ingredients together until the chickpeas are well coated. 3. Pour the chickpeas into the air fryer and spread them out in a single layer. 4. Roast for 15 minutes, stirring once halfway through the cook time.

Spicy Chicken Bites

Prep time: 10 minutes | Cook time: 10 to 12 minutes | Makes 30 bites

230 g boneless and skinless chicken thighs, cut into 30 pieces
¼ teaspoon kosher or coarse sea salt
2 tablespoons hot sauce
Cooking spray

1. Preheat the air fryer to 200°C. 2. Spray the air fryer basket with cooking spray and season the chicken bites with the salt, then place in the basket and air fry for 10 to 12 minutes or until crispy. 3. While the chicken bites cook, pour the hot sauce into a large bowl. 4. Remove the bites and add to the sauce bowl, tossing to coat. Serve warm.

Roasted Chickpeas

Prep time: 5 minutes | Cook time: 15 minutes | Makes about 1 cup

1 (425 g) can chickpeas, drained
2 teaspoons curry powder
¼ teaspoon salt
1 tablespoon olive oil

1. Drain chickpeas thoroughly and spread in a single layer on paper towels. Cover with another paper towel and press gently to remove extra moisture. Don't press too hard or you'll crush the chickpeas. 2. Mix curry powder and salt together. 3. Place chickpeas in a medium bowl and sprinkle with seasonings. Stir well to coat. 4. Add olive oil and stir again to distribute oil. 5. Air fry at 200°C for 15 minutes, stopping to shake basket about halfway through cooking time. 6. Cool completely and store in airtight container.

Black Bean Corn Dip

Prep time: 10 minutes | Cook time: 10 minutes | Serves 4

½ (425 g) can black beans, drained and rinsed
½ (425 g) can sweetcorn, drained and rinsed
60 g chunky salsa
60 g reduced-fat cream cheese, softened
30 g shredded reduced-fat Cheddar cheese
½ teaspoon ground cumin
½ teaspoon paprika
Salt and freshly ground black pepper, to taste

1. Preheat the air fryer to 164°C. 2. In a medium bowl, mix together the black beans, sweetcorn, salsa, cream cheese, Cheddar cheese, cumin, and paprikSeason with salt and pepper and stir until well combined. 3. Spoon the mixture into a baking dish. 4. Place baking dish in the air fryer basket and bake until heated through, about 10 minutes. 5. Serve hot.

Roasted Mushrooms with Garlic

Prep time: 3 minutes | Cook time: 22 to 27 minutes | Serves 4

16 garlic cloves, peeled
2 teaspoons olive oil, divided
16 button mushrooms
½ teaspoon dried marjoram
⅛ teaspoon freshly ground black pepper
1 tablespoon white wine or low-sodium vegetable stock

1. In a baking pan, mix the garlic with 1 teaspoon of olive oil. Roast in the air fryer at 176°C for 12 minutes. 2. Add the mushrooms, marjoram, and pepper. Stir to coat. Drizzle with the remaining 1 teaspoon of olive oil and the white wine. 3. Return to the air fryer and roast for 10 to 15 minutes more, or until the mushrooms and garlic cloves are tender. Serve.

Cheese Wafers

Prep time: 30 minutes | Cook time: 5 to 6 minutes per batch | Makes 4 dozen

110 g sharp Cheddar cheese, grated
60 g butter
60 g plain flour
¼ teaspoon salt
60 g crisp rice cereal
Oil for misting or cooking spray

1. Cream the butter and grated cheese together. You can do it by hand, but using a stand mixer is faster and easier. 2. Sift flour and salt together. Add it to the cheese mixture and mix until well blended. 3. Stir in cereal. 4. Place dough on wax paper and shape into a long roll about 1 inch in diameter. Wrap well with the wax paper and chill for at least 4 hours. 5. When ready to cook, preheat the air fryer to 184°C. 6. Cut cheese roll into ¼-inch slices. 7. Spray the air fryer basket with oil or cooking spray and place slices in a single layer, close but not touching. 8. Cook for 5 to 6 minutes or until golden brown. When done, place them on paper towels to cool. 9. Repeat previous step to cook remaining cheese bites.

Garlic Edamame

Prep time: 5 minutes | Cook time: 10 minutes | Serves 4

Olive oil
1 (455 g) bag frozen edamame in pods
½ teaspoon salt
½ teaspoon garlic salt
¼ teaspoon freshly ground black pepper
½ teaspoon red pepper flakes (optional)

1. Spray the air fryer basket lightly with olive oil. 2. In a medium bowl, add the frozen edamame and lightly spray with olive oil. Toss to coat. 3. In a small bowl, mix together the salt, garlic salt, black pepper, and red pepper flakes (if using). Add the mixture to the edamame and toss until evenly coated. 4. Place half the edamame in the air fryer basket. Do not overfill the basket. 5. Air fry at 192°C for 5 minutes. Shake the basket and cook until the edamame is starting to brown and get crispy, 3 to 5 more minutes. 6. Repeat with the remaining edamame and serve immediately.

Asian Rice Logs

Prep time: 30 minutes | Cook time: 5 minutes | Makes 8 rice logs

185 g cooked jasmine or sushi rice
¼ teaspoon salt
2 teaspoons five-spice powder
2 teaspoons diced shallots
1 tablespoon tamari sauce
1 egg, beaten
1 teaspoon sesame oil
2 teaspoons water
40 g plain bread crumbs
95 g panko bread crumbs
2 tablespoons sesame seeds
Orange Marmalade Dipping Sauce:
125 g all-natural orange marmalade
1 tablespoon soy sauce

1. Make the rice according to package instructions. While the rice is cooking, make the dipping sauce by combining the marmalade and soy sauce and set aside. 2. Stir together the cooked rice, salt, five-spice powder, shallots, and tamari sauce. 3. Divide rice into 8 equal pieces. With slightly damp hands, mold each piece into a log shape. Chill in freezer for 10 to 15 minutes. 4. Mix the egg, sesame oil, and water together in a shallow bowl. 5. Place the plain bread crumbs on a sheet of wax paper. 6. Mix the panko bread crumbs with the sesame seeds and place on another sheet of wax paper. 7. Roll the rice logs in plain bread crumbs, then dip in egg wash, and then dip in the panko and sesame seeds. 8. Cook the logs at 200°C for approximately 5 minutes, until golden brown. 9. Cool slightly before serving with Orange Marmalade Dipping Sauce.

Crispy Cajun Dill Pickle Chips

Prep time: 5 minutes | Cook time: 10 minutes | Makes 16 slices

30 g plain flour
60 g panko bread crumbs
1 large egg, beaten
2 teaspoons Cajun seasoning
2 large dill pickles, sliced into 8 rounds each
Cooking spray

1. Preheat the air fryer to 200°C. 2. Place the flour, panko bread crumbs, and egg into 3 separate shallow bowls, then stir the Cajun seasoning into the flour. 3. Dredge each pickle chip in the flour mixture, then the egg, and finally the bread crumbs. Shake off any excess, then place each coated pickle chip on a plate. 4. Spritz the air fryer basket with cooking spray, then place 8 pickle chips in the basket and air fry for 5 minutes, or until crispy and golden brown. Repeat this process with the remaining pickle chips. 5. Remove the chips and allow to slightly cool on a wire rack before serving.

Prawn Toasts with Sesame Seeds

Prep time: 15 minutes | Cook time: 6 to 8 minutes | Serves 4 to 6

230 g raw prawns, peeled and deveined
1 egg, beaten
2 spring onions, chopped, plus more for garnish
2 tablespoons chopped fresh coriander
2 teaspoons grated fresh ginger
1 to 2 teaspoons Sriracha sauce
1 teaspoon soy sauce
½ teaspoon toasted sesame oil
6 slices thinly sliced white sandwich bread
60 g sesame seeds
Cooking spray
Thai chilli sauce, for serving

1. Preheat the air fryer to 204°C. Spritz the air fryer basket with cooking spray. 2. In a food processor, add the prawn, egg, spring onions, coriander, ginger, Sriracha sauce, soy sauce and sesame oil, and pulse until chopped finely. You'll need to stop the food processor occasionally to scrape down the sides. Transfer the prawn mixture to a bowl. 3. On a clean work surface, cut the crusts off the sandwich bread. Using a brush, generously brush one side of each slice of bread with prawn mixture. 4. Place the sesame seeds on a plate. Press bread slices, prawn-side down, into sesame seeds to coat evenly. Cut each slice diagonally into quarters. 5. Spread the coated slices in a single layer in the air fryer basket. 6. Air fry in batches for 6 to 8 minutes, or until golden and crispy. Flip the bread slices halfway through. Repeat with the remaining bread slices. 7. Transfer to a plate and let cool for 5 minutes. Top with the chopped scallions and serve warm with Thai chilli sauce.

Vegetable Pot Stickers

Prep time: 12 minutes | Cook time: 11 to 18 minutes | Makes 12 pot stickers

125 g shredded red cabbage
30 g chopped button mushrooms
30 g grated carrot
2 tablespoons minced onion
2 garlic cloves, minced
2 teaspoons grated fresh ginger
12 gyoza/pot sticker wrappers
2½ teaspoons olive oil, divided

1. In a baking pan, combine the red cabbage, mushrooms, carrot, onion, garlic, and ginger. Add 1 tablespoon of water. Place in the air fryer and air fry at 188ºC for 3 to 6 minutes, until the vegetables are crisp-tender. Drain and set aside. 2. Working one at a time, place the pot sticker wrappers on a work surface. Top each wrapper with a scant 1 tablespoon of the filling. Fold half of the wrapper over the other half to form a half circle. Dab one edge with water and press both edges together. 3. To another pan, add 1¼ teaspoons of olive oil. Put half of the pot stickers, seam-side up, in the pan. Air fry for 5 minutes, or until the bottoms are light golden brown. Add 1 tablespoon of water and return the pan to the air fryer. 4. Air fry for 4 to 6 minutes more, or until hot. Repeat with the remaining pot stickers, remaining 1¼ teaspoons of oil, and another tablespoon of water. Serve immediately.

Homemade Sweet Potato Chips

Prep time: 5 minutes | Cook time: 15 minutes | Serves 2

1 large sweet potato, sliced thin
⅛ teaspoon salt
2 tablespoons olive oil

1. Preheat the air fryer to 192ºC. 2. In a small bowl, toss the sweet potatoes, salt, and olive oil together until the potatoes are well coated. 3. Put the sweet potato slices into the air fryer and spread them out in a single layer. 4. Fry for 10 minutes. Stir, then air fry for 3 to 5 minutes more, or until the chips reach the preferred level of crispiness.

Browned Ricotta with Capers and Lemon

Prep time: 10 minutes | Cook time: 8 to 10 minutes | Serves 4 to 6

185 g whole milk ricotta cheese
2 tablespoons extra-virgin olive oil
2 tablespoons capers, rinsed
Zest of 1 lemon, plus more for garnish
1 teaspoon finely chopped fresh rosemary
Pinch crushed red pepper flakes
Salt and freshly ground black pepper, to taste
1 tablespoon grated Parmesan cheese

1. Preheat the air fryer to 192ºC. 2. In a mixing bowl, stir together the ricotta cheese, olive oil, capers, lemon zest, rosemary, red pepper flakes, salt, and pepper until well combined. 3. Spread the mixture evenly in a baking dish and place it in the air fryer basket. 4. Air fry for 8 to 10 minutes until the top is nicely browned. 5. Remove from the basket and top with a sprinkle of grated Parmesan cheese. 6. Garnish with the lemon zest and serve warm.

Cheesy Hash Brown Bruschetta

Prep time: 5 minutes | Cook time: 6 to 8 minutes | Serves 4

4 frozen hash brown patties
1 tablespoon olive oil
40 g chopped cherry tomatoes
3 tablespoons diced fresh Mozzarella
2 tablespoons grated Parmesan cheese
1 tablespoon balsamic vinegar
1 tablespoon minced fresh basil

1. Preheat the air fryer to 204ºC. 2. Place the hash brown patties in the air fryer in a single layer. Air fry for 6 to 8 minutes, or until the potatoes are crisp, hot, and golden brown. 3. Meanwhile, combine the olive oil, tomatoes, Mozzarella, Parmesan, vinegar, and basil in a small bowl. 4. When the potatoes are done, carefully remove from the basket and arrange on a serving plate. Top with the tomato mixture and serve.

Peppery Chicken Meatballs

Prep time: 5 minutes | Cook time: 13 to 20 minutes | Makes 16 meatballs

2 teaspoons olive oil
30 g minced onion
30 g minced red bell pepper
2 vanilla or plain wafers, crushed
1 egg white
½ teaspoon dried thyme
230 g minced chicken breast

1. Preheat the air fryer to 188ºC. 2. In a baking pan, mix the olive oil, onion, and red bell pepper. Put the pan in the air fryer. Air fry for 3 to 5 minutes, or until the vegetables are tender. 3. In a medium bowl, mix the cooked vegetables, crushed wafers, egg white, and thyme until well combined 4. Mix in the chicken, gently but thoroughly, until everything is combined. 5. Form the mixture into 16 meatballs and place them in the air fryer basket. Air fry for 10 to 15 minutes, or until the meatballs reach an internal temperature of 76ºC on a meat thermometer. 6. Serve immediately.

Rumaki

Prep time: 30 minutes | Cook time: 10 to 12 minutes per batch | Makes about 24 rumaki

280 g raw chicken livers
1 can sliced water chestnuts, drained
60 g low-sodium teriyaki sauce
12 slices turkey bacon

1. Cut livers into 1½-inch pieces, trimming out tough veins as you slice. 2. Place livers, water chestnuts, and teriyaki sauce in small container with lid. If needed, add another tablespoon of teriyaki sauce to make sure livers are covered. Refrigerate for 1 hour. 3. When ready to cook, cut bacon slices in half crosswise. 4. Wrap 1 piece of liver and 1 slice of water chestnut in each bacon strip. Secure with toothpick. 5. When you have wrapped half of the livers, place them in the air fryer basket in a single layer. 6. Air fry at 200ºC for 10 to 12 minutes, until liver is done and bacon is crispy. 7. While first batch cooks, wrap the remaining livers. Repeat step 6 to cook your second batch.

Cheese Drops

Prep time: 15 minutes | Cook time: 10 minutes per batch | Serves 8

95 g plain flour
½ teaspoon kosher or coarse sea salt
¼ teaspoon cayenne pepper
¼ teaspoon smoked paprika
¼ teaspoon black pepper
Dash garlic powder (optional)
60 g butter, softened
125 g shredded sharp Cheddar cheese, at room temperature
Olive oil spray

1. In a small bowl, combine the flour, salt, cayenne, paprika, pepper, and garlic powder, if using. 2. Using a food processor, cream the butter and cheese until smooth. Gently add the seasoned flour and process until the dough is well combined, smooth, and no longer sticky. (Or make the dough in a stand mixer fitted with the paddle attachment: Cream the butter and cheese on medium speed until smooth, then add the seasoned flour and beat at low speed until smooth.) 3. Divide the dough into 32 equal-size pieces. On a lightly floured surface, roll each piece into a small ball. 4. Spray the air fryer basket with oil spray. Arrange 16 cheese drops in the basket. Set the air fryer to 164ºC for 10 minutes, or until drops are just starting to brown. Transfer to a wire rack. Repeat with remaining dough, checking for doneness at 8 minutes. 5. Cool the cheese drops completely on the wire rack. Store in an airtight container until ready to serve, or up to 1 or 2 days.

Golden Onion Rings

Prep time: 15 minutes | Cook time: 14 minutes per batch | Serves 4

1 large white onion, peeled and cut into ½ to ¾-inch-thick slices
125 ml skimmed milk
125 g whole-wheat pastry flour, or plain flour
2 tablespoons cornflour
¾ teaspoon sea salt, divided
½ teaspoon freshly ground black pepper, divided
¾ teaspoon granulated garlic, divided
185 g whole grain bread crumbs, or gluten-free bread crumbs
Cooking oil spray (coconut, sunflower, or safflower)
Ketchup, for serving (optional)

1. Carefully separate the onion slices into rings—a gentle touch is important here. 2. Place the milk in a shallow bowl and set aside. 3. Make the first breading: In a medium bowl, stir together the flour, cornflour, ¼ teaspoon of salt, ¼ teaspoon of pepper, and ¼ teaspoon of granulated garlic. Set aside. 4. Make the second breading: In a separate medium bowl, stir together the bread crumbs with the remaining ½ teaspoon of salt, the remaining ½ teaspoon of garlic, and the remaining ½ teaspoon of pepper. Set aside. 5. Insert the crisper plate into the basket and the basket into the unit. Preheat the unit by selecting AIR FRY, setting the temperature to 200ºC, and setting the time to 3 minutes. Select START/STOP to begin. 6. Once the unit is preheated, spray the crisper plate and the basket with cooking oil. 7. To make the onion rings, dip one ring into the milk and into the first breading mixture. Dip the ring into the milk again and back into the first breading mixture, coating thoroughly. Dip the ring into the milk one last time and then into the second breading mixture, coating thoroughly. Gently lay the onion ring in the basket. Repeat with additional rings and, as you place them into the basket, do not overlap them too much. Once all the onion rings are in the basket, generously spray the tops with cooking oil. 8. Select AIR FRY, set the temperature to 200ºC, and set the time to 14 minutes. Insert the basket into the unit. Select START/STOP to begin. 9. After 4 minutes, open the unit and spray the rings generously with cooking oil. Close the unit to resume cooking. After 3 minutes, remove the basket and spray the onion rings again. Remove the rings, turn them over, and place them back into the basket. Generously spray them again with oil. Reinsert the basket to resume cooking. After 4 minutes, generously spray the rings with oil one last time. Resume cooking for the remaining 3 minutes, or until the onion rings are very crunchy and brown. 10. When the cooking is complete, serve the hot rings with ketchup, or other sauce of choice.

Lemony Pear Chips

Prep time: 15 minutes | Cook time: 9 to 13 minutes | Serves 4

2 firm Bosc pears, cut crosswise into ⅛-inch-thick slices
1 tablespoon freshly squeezed lemon juice
½ teaspoon ground cinnamon
⅛ teaspoon ground cardamom

1. Preheat the air fryer to 192ºC. 2. Separate the smaller stem-end pear rounds from the larger rounds with seeds. Remove the core and seeds from the larger slices. Sprinkle all slices with lemon juice, cinnamon, and cardamom. 3. Put the smaller chips into the air fryer basket. Air fry for 3 to 5 minutes, or until light golden brown, shaking the basket once during cooking. Remove from the air fryer. 4. Repeat with the larger slices, air frying for 6 to 8 minutes, or until light golden brown, shaking the basket once during cooking. 5. Remove the chips from the air fryer. Cool and serve or store in an airtight container at room temperature up for to 2 days.

Parmesan French Fries

Prep time: 10 minutes | Cook time: 25 minutes | Serves 2 to 3

2 to 3 large russet potatoes, peeled and cut into ½-inch sticks
2 teaspoons vegetable or canola oil
95 g grated Parmesan cheese
½ teaspoon salt
Freshly ground black pepper, to taste
1 teaspoon fresh chopped parsley

1. Bring a large saucepan of salted water to a boil on the stovetop while you peel and cut the potatoes. Blanch the potatoes in the boiling salted water for 4 minutes while you preheat the air fryer to 204ºC. Strain the potatoes and rinse them with cold water. Dry them well with a clean kitchen towel. 2. Toss the dried potato sticks gently with the oil and place them in the air fryer basket. Air fry for 25 minutes, shaking the basket a few times while the fries cook to help them brown evenly. 3. Combine the Parmesan cheese, salt and pepper. With 2 minutes left on the air fryer cooking time, sprinkle the fries with the Parmesan cheese mixture. Toss the fries to coat them evenly with the cheese mixture and continue to air fry for the final 2 minutes, until the cheese has melted and just starts to brown. Sprinkle the finished fries with chopped parsley, a little more grated Parmesan cheese if you like, and serve.

Classic Spring Rolls

Prep time: 10 minutes | Cook time: 9 minutes | Makes 16 spring rolls

4 teaspoons toasted sesame oil
6 medium garlic cloves, minced or pressed
1 tablespoon grated peeled fresh ginger
250 g thinly sliced shiitake mushrooms
500 g chopped green or Savoy cabbage
125 g grated carrot
½ teaspoon sea salt
16 rice paper wrappers
Cooking oil spray (sunflower, safflower, or refined coconut)
Gluten-free sweet and sour sauce or Thai sweet chilli sauce, for serving (optional)

1. Place a wok or sauté pan over medium heat until hot. 2. Add the sesame oil, garlic, ginger, mushrooms, cabbage, carrot, and salt. Cook for 3 to 4 minutes, stirring often, until the cabbage is lightly wilted. Remove the pan from the heat. 3. Gently run a rice paper under water. Lay it on a flat nonabsorbent surface. Place about 60 g cabbage filling in the middle. Once the wrapper is soft enough to roll, fold the bottom up over the filling, fold in the sides, and roll the wrapper all the way up. (Basically, make a tiny burrito.) 4. Repeat step 3 to make the remaining spring rolls until you have the number of spring rolls you want to cook right now (and the amount that will fit in the air fryer basket in a single layer without them touching each other). Refrigerate any leftover filling in an airtight container for about 1 week. 5. Insert the crisper plate into the basket and the basket into the unit. Preheat the unit by selecting AIR FRY, setting the temperature to 200°C, and setting the time to 3 minutes. Select START/STOP to begin. 6. Once the unit is preheated, spray the crisper plate and the basket with cooking oil. Place the spring rolls into the basket, leaving a little room between them so they don't stick to each other. Spray the top of each spring roll with cooking oil. 7. Select AIR FRY, set the temperature to 200°C, and set the time to 9 minutes. Select START/STOP to begin. 8. When the cooking is complete, the egg rolls should be crisp-ish and lightly browned. Serve immediately, plain or with a sauce of choice.

Asian Five-Spice Wings

Prep time: 30 minutes | Cook time: 13 to 15 minutes | Serves 4

910 g chicken wings
125 g Asian-style salad dressing
2 tablespoons Chinese five-spice powder

1. Cut off wing tips and discard or freeze for stock. Cut remaining wing pieces in two at the joint. 2. Place wing pieces in a large sealable plastic bag. Pour in the Asian dressing, seal bag, and massage the marinade into the wings until well coated. Refrigerate for at least an hour. 3. Remove wings from bag, drain off excess marinade, and place wings in air fryer basket. 4. Air fry at 184°C for 13 to 15 minutes or until juices run clear. About halfway through cooking time, shake the basket or stir wings for more even cooking. 5. Transfer cooked wings to plate in a single layer. Sprinkle half of the Chinese five-spice powder on the wings, turn, and sprinkle other side with remaining seasoning.

Dark Chocolate and Cranberry Granola Bars

Prep time: 5 minutes | Cook time: 15 minutes | Serves 6

250 g certified gluten-free quick oats
2 tablespoons sugar-free dark chocolate chunks
2 tablespoons unsweetened dried cranberries
3 tablespoons unsweetened desiccated coconut
125 g raw honey
1 teaspoon ground cinnamon
⅛ teaspoon salt
2 tablespoons olive oil

1. Preheat the air fryer to 184°C. Line an 8-by-8-inch baking dish with baking paper that comes up the side so you can lift it out after cooking. 2. In a large bowl, mix together all of the ingredients until well combined. 3. Press the oat mixture into the pan in an even layer. 4. Place the pan into the air fryer basket and bake for 15 minutes. 5. Remove the pan from the air fryer, and lift the granola cake out of the pan using the edges of the baking paper. 6. Allow to cool for 5 minutes before slicing into 6 equal bars. 7. Serve immediately, or wrap in plastic wrap and store at room temperature for up to 1 week.

Bruschetta with Basil Pesto

Prep time: 10 minutes | Cook time: 5 to 11 minutes | Serves 4

8 slices French bread, ½ inch thick
2 tablespoons softened butter
125 g shredded Mozzarella cheese
125 g basil pesto
125 g chopped grape tomatoes
2 spring onions, thinly sliced

1. Preheat the air fryer to 176°C. 2. Spread the bread with the butter and place butter-side up in the air fryer basket. Bake for 3 to 5 minutes, or until the bread is light golden brown. 3. Remove the bread from the basket and top each piece with some of the cheese. Return to the basket in 2 batches and bake for 1 to 3 minutes, or until the cheese melts. 4. Meanwhile, combine the pesto, tomatoes, and spring onions in a small bowl. 5. When the cheese has melted, remove the bread from the air fryer and place on a serving plate. Top each slice with some of the pesto mixture and serve.

Ranch Oyster Snack Crackers

Prep time: 3 minutes | Cook time: 12 minutes | Serves 6

Oil, for spraying
65 ml olive oil
2 teaspoons dry ranch seasoning
1 teaspoon chilli powder
½ teaspoon dried dill
½ teaspoon garlic granules
½ teaspoon salt
1 (255 g) bag oyster crackers

1. Preheat the air fryer to 164°C. Line the air fryer basket with baking paper and spray lightly with oil. 2. In a large bowl, mix together the olive oil, ranch seasoning, chilli powder, dill, garlic, and salt. Add the crackers and toss until evenly coated. 3. Place the mixture in the prepared basket. 4. Cook for 10 to 12 minutes, shaking or stirring every 3 to 4 minutes, or until crisp and golden brown.

Crunchy Chickpeas

Prep time: 5 minutes | Cook time: 15 to 20 minutes | Serves 4

½ teaspoon chilli powder	1 (540 g) can chickpeas, drained and rinsed
½ teaspoon ground cumin	
¼ teaspoon cayenne pepper	Cooking spray
¼ teaspoon salt	

1. Preheat the air fryer to 200°C. Lightly spritz the air fryer basket with cooking spray. 2. Mix the chilli powder, cumin, cayenne pepper, and salt in a small bowl. 3. Place the chickpeas in a medium bowl and lightly mist with cooking spray. 4. Add the spice mixture to the chickpeas and toss until evenly coated. 5. Place the chickpeas in the air fryer basket and air fry for 15 to 20 minutes, or until the chickpeas are cooked to your preferred crunchiness. Shake the basket three or four times during cooking. 6. Let the chickpeas cool for 5 minutes before serving.

Stuffed Figs with Goat Cheese and Honey

Prep time: 5 minutes | Cook time: 10 minutes | Serves 4

8 fresh figs	1 tablespoon honey, plus more for serving
60 g goat cheese	
¼ teaspoon ground cinnamon	1 tablespoon olive oil

1. Preheat the air fryer to 184°C. 2. Cut the stem off of each fig. 3. Cut an X into the top of each fig, cutting halfway down the fig. Leave the base intact. 4. In a small bowl, mix together the goat cheese, cinnamon, and honey. 5. Spoon the goat cheese mixture into the cavity of each fig. 6. Place the figs in a single layer in the air fryer basket. Drizzle the olive oil over top of the figs and roast for 10 minutes. 7. Serve with an additional drizzle of honey.

Courgette Fries with Roasted Garlic Aïoli

Prep time: 20 minutes | Cook time: 12 minutes | Serves 4

1 tablespoon vegetable oil	Courgette Fries:
½ head green or savoy cabbage, finely shredded	60 g plain flour
	2 eggs, beaten
Roasted Garlic Aïoli:	125 g seasoned bread crumbs
1 teaspoon roasted garlic	Salt and pepper, to taste
125 g mayonnaise	1 large courgette, cut into ½-inch sticks
2 tablespoons olive oil	
Juice of ½ lemon	Olive oil
Salt and pepper, to taste	

1. Make the aïoli: Combine the roasted garlic, mayonnaise, olive oil and lemon juice in a bowl and whisk well. Season the aïoli with salt and pepper to taste. 2. Prepare the courgette fries. Create a dredging station with three shallow dishes. Place the flour in the first shallow dish and season well with salt and freshly ground black pepper. Put the beaten eggs in the second shallow dish. In the third shallow dish, combine the bread crumbs, salt and pepper. Dredge the courgette sticks, coating with flour first, then dipping them into the eggs to coat, and finally tossing in bread crumbs. Shake the dish with the bread crumbs and pat the crumbs onto the courgette sticks gently with your hands so they stick evenly. 3. Place the courgette fries on a flat surface and let them sit at least 10 minutes before air frying to let them dry out a little. Preheat the air fryer to 204°C. 4. Spray the courgette sticks with olive oil, and place them into the air fryer basket. You can air fry the courgette in two layers, placing the second layer in the opposite direction to the first. Air fry for 12 minutes turning and rotating the fries halfway through the cooking time. Spray with additional oil when you turn them over. 5. Serve courgette fries warm with the roasted garlic aïoli.

Caramelised Onion Dip

Prep time: 5 minutes | Cook time: 30 minutes | Serves 8 to 10

1 tablespoon butter	125 g sour cream
1 medium yellow onion, halved and thinly sliced	¼ teaspoon onion powder
	1 tablespoon chopped fresh chives
¼ teaspoon kosher or coarse sea salt, plus additional for seasoning	Black pepper, to taste
	Thick-cut potato chips or vegetable chips
110 g cream cheese, softened	

1. Place the butter in a baking pan. Place the pan in the air fryer basket. Set the air fryer to 92°C for 1 minute, or until the butter is melted. Add the onions and salt to the pan. 2. Set the air fryer to 92°C for 15 minutes, or until onions are softened. Set the air fryer to 192°C for 15 minutes, until onions are a deep golden brown, stirring two or three times during the cooking time. Let cool completely. 3. In a medium bowl, stir together the cooked onions, cream cheese, sour cream, onion powder, and chives. Season with salt and pepper. Cover and refrigerate for 2 hours to allow the flavors to blend. 4. Serve the dip with potato chips or vegetable chips.

Old Bay Chicken Wings

Prep time: 10 minutes | Cook time: 12 to 15 minutes | Serves 4

2 tablespoons Old Bay seasoning	2 teaspoons salt
	910 g chicken wings, patted dry
2 teaspoons baking powder	Cooking spray

1. Preheat the air fryer to 204°C. Lightly spray the air fryer basket with cooking spray. 2. Combine the Old Bay seasoning, baking powder, and salt in a large sandwich bag. Add the chicken wings, seal, and shake until the wings are thoroughly coated in the seasoning mixture. 3. Lay the chicken wings in the air fryer basket in a single layer and lightly mist with cooking spray. You may need to work in batches to avoid overcrowding. 4. Air fry for 12 to 15 minutes, flipping the wings halfway through, or until the wings are lightly browned and the internal temperature reaches at least 76°C on a meat thermometer. 5. Remove from the basket to a plate and repeat with the remaining chicken wings. 6. Serve hot.

Chapter 8 Desserts

Honeyed Roasted Apples with Walnuts

Prep time: 5 minutes | Cook time: 12 to 15 minutes | Serves 4

2 Granny Smith apples
30 g certified gluten-free rolled oats
2 tablespoons honey
½ teaspoon ground cinnamon
2 tablespoons chopped walnuts
Pinch salt
1 tablespoon olive oil

1. Preheat the air fryer to 192°C. 2. Core the apples and slice them in half. 3. In a medium bowl, mix together the oats, honey, cinnamon, walnuts, salt, and olive oil. 4. Scoop a quarter of the oat mixture onto the top of each half apple. 5. Place the apples in the air fryer basket, and roast for 12 to 15 minutes, or until the apples are fork-tender.

Blackberry Cobbler

Prep time: 15 minutes | Cook time: 25 to 30 minutes | Serves 6

375 g fresh or frozen blackberries
220 g sugar, divided
1 teaspoon vanilla extract
8 tablespoons butter, melted
125 g self-raising flour
1 to 2 tablespoons oil

1. In a medium bowl, stir together the blackberries, 125 g sugar, and vanill2. In another medium bowl, stir together the melted butter, remaining 95 g sugar, and flour until a dough forms. 3. Spritz a baking pan with oil. Add the blackberry mixture. Crumble the flour mixture over the fruit. Cover the pan with aluminum foil. 4. Preheat the air fryer to 176°C. 5. Place the covered pan in the air fryer basket. Cook for 20 to 25 minutes until the filling is thickened. 6. Uncover the pan and cook for 5 minutes more, depending on how juicy and browned you like your cobbler. Let sit for 5 minutes before serving.

Cinnamon and Pecan Pie

Prep time: 10 minutes | Cook time: 25 minutes | Serves 4

1 pie case
½ teaspoons cinnamon
¾ teaspoon vanilla extract
2 eggs
185 g maple syrup
⅛ teaspoon nutmeg
3 tablespoons melted butter, divided
2 tablespoons sugar
60 g chopped pecans

1. Preheat the air fryer to 188°C. 2. In a small bowl, coat the pecans in 1 tablespoon of melted butter. 3. Transfer the pecans to the air fryer and air fry for about 10 minutes. 4. Put the pie dough in a greased pie pan and add the pecans on top. 5. In a bowl, mix the rest of the ingredients. Pour this over the pecans. 6. Put the pan in the air fryer and bake for 25 minutes. 7. Serve immediately.

Olive Oil Cake

Prep time: 10 minutes | Cook time: 30 minutes | Serves 8

250 g blanched finely ground almond flour
5 large eggs, whisked
185 ml extra-virgin olive oil
40 g granulated sweetener
1 teaspoon vanilla extract
1 teaspoon baking powder

1. In a large bowl, mix all ingredients. Pour batter into an ungreased round nonstick baking dish. 2. Place dish into air fryer basket. Adjust the temperature to 148°C and bake for 30 minutes. The cake will be golden on top and firm in the center when done. 3. Let cake cool in dish 30 minutes before slicing and serving.

Mini Cheesecake

Prep time: 10 minutes | Cook time: 15 minutes | Serves 2

60 g walnuts
2 tablespoons salted butter
2 tablespoons granulated sweetener
110 g full-fat cream cheese, softened
1 large egg
½ teaspoon vanilla extract
15 g powdered sweetener

1. Place walnuts, butter, and granulated sweetener in a food processor. Pulse until ingredients stick together and a dough forms. 2. Press dough into a spring-form pan then place the pan into the air fryer basket. 3. Adjust the temperature to 204°C and bake for 5 minutes. 4. When done, remove the crust and let cool. 5. In a medium bowl, mix cream cheese with egg, vanilla extract, and powdered sweetener until smooth. 6. Spoon mixture on top of baked walnut crust and place into the air fryer basket. 7. Adjust the temperature to 148°C and bake for 10 minutes. 8. Once done, chill for 2 hours before serving.

Courgette Bread

Prep time: 10 minutes | Cook time: 40 minutes | Serves 12

250 g coconut flour
2 teaspoons baking powder
95 g granulated sweetener
125 ml coconut oil, melted
1 teaspoon apple cider vinegar
1 teaspoon vanilla extract
3 eggs, beaten
1 courgette, grated
1 teaspoon ground cinnamon

1. In the mixing bowl, mix coconut flour with baking powder, sweetener, coconut oil, apple cider vinegar, vanilla extract, eggs, courgette, and ground cinnamon. 2. Transfer the mixture into the air fryer basket and flatten it in the shape of the bread. 3. Cook the bread at 176°C for 40 minutes.

Chocolate Chip-Pecan Biscotti

Prep time: 15 minutes | Cook time: 20 to 22 minutes | Serves 10

160 g finely ground blanched almond flour
¾ teaspoon baking powder
½ teaspoon xanthan gum
¼ teaspoon sea salt
3 tablespoons unsalted butter, at room temperature
40 g powdered sweetener
1 large egg, beaten
1 teaspoon pure vanilla extract
40 g chopped pecans
30 g stevia-sweetened chocolate chips, such as Lily's Sweets brand
Melted organic chocolate chips and chopped pecans, for topping (optional)

1. In a large bowl, combine the almond flour, baking powder, xanthan gum, and salt. 2. Line a cake pan that fits inside your air fryer with baking paper. 3. In the bowl of a stand mixer, beat together the butter and sweetener. Add the beaten egg and vanilla, and beat for about 3 minutes. 4. Add the almond flour mixture to the butter-and-egg mixture; beat until just combined. 5. Stir in the pecans and chocolate chips. 6. Transfer the dough to the prepared pan, and press it into the bottom. 7. Set the air fryer to 164ºC and bake for 12 minutes. Remove from the air fryer and let cool for 15 minutes. Using a sharp knife, cut the cookie into thin strips, then return the strips to the cake pan with the bottom sides facing up. 8. Set the air fryer to 148ºC. Bake for 8 to 10 minutes. 9. Remove from the air fryer and let cool completely on a wire rack. If desired, dip one side of each biscotti piece into melted chocolate chips, and top with chopped pecans.

Glazed Cherry Turnovers

Prep time: 10 minutes | Cook time: 14 minutes per batch | Serves 8

2 sheets frozen puff pastry, thawed
1 (600 g) can premium cherry pie filling
2 teaspoons ground cinnamon
1 egg, beaten
125 g sliced almonds
125 g icing sugar
2 tablespoons milk

1. Roll a sheet of puff pastry out into a square that is approximately 10-inches by 10-inches. Cut this large square into quarters. 2. Mix the cherry pie filling and cinnamon together in a bowl. Spoon 60 g cherry filling into the center of each puff pastry square. Brush the perimeter of the pastry square with the egg wash. Fold one corner of the puff pastry over the cherry pie filling towards the opposite corner, forming a triangle. Seal the two edges of the pastry together with the tip of a fork, making a design with the tines. Brush the top of the turnovers with the egg wash and sprinkle sliced almonds over each one. Repeat these steps with the second sheet of puff pastry. You should have eight turnovers at the end. 3. Preheat the air fryer to 188ºC. 4. Air fry two turnovers at a time for 14 minutes, carefully turning them over halfway through the cooking time. 5. While the turnovers are cooking, make the glaze by whisking the icing sugar and milk together in a small bowl until smooth. Let the glaze sit for a minute so the sugar can absorb the milk. If the consistency is still too thick to drizzle, add a little more milk, a drop at a time, and stir until smooth. 6. Let the cooked cherry turnovers sit for at least 10 minutes. Then drizzle the glaze over each turnover in a zig-zag motion. Serve warm or at room temperature.

Mini Peanut Butter Tarts

Prep time: 25 minutes | Cook time: 12 to 15 minutes | Serves 8

125 g pecans
125 g finely ground blanched almond flour
2 tablespoons unsalted butter, at room temperature
90 g powdered sweetener, divided
125 g heavy (whipping) cream
2 tablespoons mascarpone cheese
110 g cream cheese
125 g sugar-free peanut butter
1 teaspoon pure vanilla extract
⅛ teaspoon sea salt
60 g organic chocolate chips
1 tablespoon coconut oil
30 g chopped peanuts or pecans

1. Place the pecans in the bowl of a food processor; process until they are finely ground. 2. Transfer the ground pecans to a medium bowl and stir in the almond flour. Add the butter and 2 tablespoons of sweetener, and stir until the mixture becomes wet and crumbly. 3. Divide the mixture among 8 silicone muffin cups, pressing the crust firmly with your fingers into the bottom and part way up the sides of each cup. 4. Arrange the muffin cups in the air fryer basket, working in batches if necessary. Set the air fryer to 148ºC and bake for 12 to 15 minutes, until the crusts begin to brown. Remove the cups from the air fryer and set them aside to cool. 5. In the bowl of a stand mixer, combine the heavy cream and mascarpone cheese. Beat until peaks form. Transfer to a large bowl. 6. In the same stand mixer bowl, combine the cream cheese, peanut butter, remaining 60 g sweetener, vanilla, and salt. Beat at medium-high speed until smooth. 7. Reduce the speed to low and add the heavy cream mixture back a spoonful at a time, beating after each addition. 8. Spoon the peanut butter mixture over the crusts, and freeze the tarts for 30 minutes. 9. Place the chocolate chips and coconut oil in the top of a double boiler over high heat. Stir until melted, then remove from the heat. 10. Drizzle the melted chocolate over the peanut butter tarts. Top with the chopped nuts and freeze the tarts for another 15 minutes, until set. 11. Store the peanut butter tarts in an airtight container in the refrigerator for up to 1 week or in the freezer for up to 1 month.

Lime Bars

Prep time: 10 minutes | Cook time: 33 minutes | Makes 12 bars

185 g blanched finely ground almond flour, divided
95 g powdered sweetener, divided
4 tablespoons salted butter, melted
125 ml fresh lime juice
2 large eggs, whisked

1. In a medium bowl, mix together 125 g flour, 30 g sweetener, and butter. Press mixture into bottom of an ungreased round nonstick cake pan. 2. Place pan into air fryer basket. Adjust the temperature to 148ºC and bake for 13 minutes. Crust will be brown and set in the middle when done. 3. Allow to cool in pan 10 minutes. 4. In a medium bowl, combine remaining flour, remaining sweetener, lime juice, and eggs. Pour mixture over cooled crust and return to air fryer for 20 minutes at 148ºC. Top will be browned and firm when done. 5. Let cool completely in pan, about 30 minutes, then chill covered in the refrigerator 1 hour. Serve chilled.

Eggless Farina Cake

Prep time: 30 minutes | Cook time: 25 minutes | Serves 6

Vegetable oil
500 ml hot water
125 g chopped dried fruit, such as apricots, golden raisins, figs, and/or dates
125 g farina (or very fine semolina)
250 ml milk
125 g sugar
30 g ghee, butter, or coconut oil, melted
2 tablespoons plain Greek yogurt or sour cream
1 teaspoon ground cardamom
1 teaspoon baking powder
½ teaspoon baking soda
Whipped cream, for serving

1. Grease a baking pan with vegetable oil. 2. In a small bowl, combine the hot water and dried fruit; set aside for 20 minutes to plump the fruit. 3. Meanwhile, in a large bowl, whisk together the farina, milk, sugar, ghee, yogurt, and cardamom. Let stand for 20 minutes to allow the farina to soften and absorb some of the liquid. 4. Drain the dried fruit and gently stir it into the batter. Add the baking powder and baking soda and stir until thoroughly combined. 5. Pour the batter into the prepared pan. Set the pan in the air fryer basket. Set the air fryer to 164ºC for 25 minutes, or until a toothpick inserted into the center of the cake comes out clean. 6. Let the cake cool in the pan on a wire rack for 10 minutes. Remove the cake from the pan and let cool on the rack for 20 minutes before slicing. 7. Slice and serve topped with whipped cream.

Grilled Pineapple Dessert

Prep time: 5 minutes | Cook time: 12 minutes | Serves 4

Oil for misting or cooking spray
4 ½-inch-thick slices fresh pineapple, core removed
1 tablespoon honey
¼ teaspoon brandy or apple juice
2 tablespoons slivered almonds, toasted
Vanilla frozen yogurt or coconut sorbet

1. Spray both sides of pineapple slices with oil or cooking spray. Place into air fryer basket. 2. Air fry at 200ºC for 6 minutes. Turn slices over and cook for an additional 6 minutes. 3. Mix together the honey and brandy. 4. Remove cooked pineapple slices from air fryer, sprinkle with toasted almonds, and drizzle with honey mixture. 5. Serve with a scoop of frozen yogurt or sorbet on the side.

Coconut Muffins

Prep time: 5 minutes | Cook time: 25 minutes | Serves 5

60 g coconut flour
2 tablespoons cocoa powder
3 tablespoons granulated sweetener
1 teaspoon baking powder
2 tablespoons coconut oil
2 eggs, beaten
60 g desiccated coconut

1. In the mixing bowl, mix all ingredients. 2. Then pour the mixture into the molds of the muffin and transfer in the air fryer basket. 3. Cook the muffins at 176ºC for 25 minutes.

Apple Hand Pies

Prep time: 15 minutes | Cook time: 25 minutes | Serves 8

2 apples, cored and diced
60 g honey
1 teaspoon ground cinnamon
1 teaspoon vanilla extract
⅛ teaspoon ground nutmeg
2 teaspoons cornflour
1 teaspoon water
4 refrigerated piecrusts
Cooking oil spray

1. Insert the crisper plate into the basket and the basket into the unit. Preheat the unit by selecting AIR FRY, setting the temperature to 204ºC, and setting the time to 3 minutes. Select START/STOP to begin. 2. In a metal bowl that fits into the basket, stir together the apples, honey, cinnamon, vanilla, and nutmeg. 3. In a small bowl, whisk the cornflour and water until the cornflour dissolves. 4. Once the unit is preheated, place the metal bowl with the apples into the basket. 5. Select AIR FRY, set the temperature to 204ºC, and set the time to 5 minutes. Select START/STOP to begin. 6. After 2 minutes, stir the apples. Resume cooking for 2 minutes. 7. Remove the bowl and stir the cornflour mixture into the apples. Reinsert the metal bowl into the basket and resume cooking for about 30 seconds until the sauce thickens slightly. 8. When the cooking is complete, refrigerate the apples while you prepare the piecrust. 9. Cut each piecrust into 2 (4-inch) circles. You should have 8 circles of crust. 10. Lay the piecrusts on a work surface. Divide the apple filling among the piecrusts, mounding the mixture in the center of each round. 11. Fold each piecrust over so the top layer of crust is about an inch short of the bottom layer. (The edges should not meet.) Use the back of a fork to seal the edges. 12. Insert the crisper plate into the basket and the basket into the unit. Preheat the unit by selecting AIR FRY, setting the temperature to 204ºC, and setting the time to 3 minutes. Select START/STOP to begin. 13. Once the unit is preheated, spray the crisper plate with cooking oil, line the basket with baking paper, and spray it with cooking oil. Working in batches, place the hand pies into the basket in a single layer. 14. Select AIR FRY, set the temperature to 204ºC, and set the time to 10 minutes. Select START/STOP to begin. 15. When the cooking is complete, let the hand pies cool for 5 minutes before removing from the basket. 16. Repeat steps 13, 14, and 15 with the remaining pies.

Pecan and Cherry Stuffed Apples

Prep time: 10 minutes | Cook time: 20 minutes | Serves 4

4 apples (about 570 g)
30 g chopped pecans
40 g dried tart cherries
1 tablespoon melted butter
3 tablespoons brown sugar
¼ teaspoon allspice
Pinch salt
Ice cream, for serving

1. Cut off top ½ inch from each apple; reserve tops. With a melon baller, core through stem ends without breaking through the bottom. (Do not trim bases.) 2. Preheat the air fryer to 176ºC. Combine pecans, cherries, butter, brown sugar, allspice, and a pinch of salt. Stuff mixture into the hollow centers of the apples. Cover with apple tops. Put in the air fryer basket, using tongs. Air fry for 20 to 25 minutes, or just until tender. 3. Serve warm with ice cream.

Lemon Raspberry Muffins

Prep time: 5 minutes | Cook time: 15 minutes | Serves 6

250 g almond flour
95 g powdered sweetener
1¼ teaspoons baking powder
⅓ teaspoon ground allspice
⅓ teaspoon ground star anise
½ teaspoon grated lemon zest
¼ teaspoon salt
2 eggs
250 g sour cream
125 ml coconut oil
60 g raspberries

1. Preheat the air fryer to 176°C. Line a muffin pan with 6 paper liners. 2. In a mixing bowl, mix the almond flour, sweetener, baking powder, allspice, star anise, lemon zest, and salt. 3. In another mixing bowl, beat the eggs, sour cream, and coconut oil until well mixed. Add the egg mixture to the flour mixture and stir to combine. Mix in the raspberries. 4. Scrape the batter into the prepared muffin cups, filling each about three-quarters full. 5. Bake for 15 minutes, or until the tops are golden and a toothpick inserted in the middle comes out clean. 6. Allow the muffins to cool for 10 minutes in the muffin pan before removing and serving.

Bananas Foster

Prep time: 5 minutes | Cook time: 7 minutes | Serves 2

1 tablespoon unsalted butter
2 teaspoons dark brown sugar
1 banana, peeled and halved lengthwise and then crosswise
2 tablespoons chopped pecans
⅛ teaspoon ground cinnamon
2 tablespoons light rum
Vanilla ice cream, for serving

1. In a baking pan, combine the butter and brown sugar. Place the pan in the air fryer basket. Set the air fryer to 176°C for 2 minutes, or until the butter and sugar are melted. Swirl to combine. 2. Add the banana pieces and pecans, turning the bananas to coat. Set the air fryer to 176°C for 5 minutes, turning the banana pieces halfway through the cooking time. Sprinkle with the cinnamon. 3. Remove the pan from the air fryer and place on an unlit stovetop for safety. Add the rum to the pan, swirling to combine it with the butter mixture. Carefully light the sauce with a long-reach lighter. Spoon the flaming sauce over the banana pieces until the flames die out. 4. Serve the warm bananas and sauce over vanilla ice cream.

Pears with Honey-Lemon Ricotta

Prep time: 10 minutes | Cook time: 8 minutes | Serves 4

2 large Bartlett pears
3 tablespoons butter, melted
3 tablespoons brown sugar
½ teaspoon ground ginger
¼ teaspoon ground cardamom
60 g whole-milk ricotta cheese
1 tablespoon honey, plus additional for drizzling
1 teaspoon pure almond extract
1 teaspoon pure lemon extract

1. Peel each pear and cut in half lengthwise. Use a melon baller to scoop out the core. Place the pear halves in a medium bowl, add the melted butter, and toss. Add the brown sugar, ginger, and cardamom; toss to coat. 2. Place the pear halves, cut side down, in the air fryer basket. Set the air fryer to 192°C for 8 to 10 minutes, or until the pears are lightly browned and tender, but not mushy. 3. Meanwhile, in a medium bowl, combine the ricotta, honey, and almond and lemon extracts. Beat with an electric mixer on medium speed until the mixture is light and fluffy, about 1 minute. 4. To serve, divide the ricotta mixture among four small shallow bowls. Place a pear half, cut side up, on top of the cheese. Drizzle with additional honey and serve.

Courgette Nut Muffins

Prep time: 15 minutes | Cook time: 15 minutes | Serves 4

65 ml vegetable oil, plus more for greasing
95 g plain flour
¾ teaspoon ground cinnamon
¼ teaspoon kosher or coarse sea salt
¼ teaspoon baking soda
¼ teaspoon baking powder
2 large eggs
60 g sugar
60 g grated courgette
30 g chopped walnuts

1. Generously grease four 110 g ramekins or a baking pan with vegetable oil. 2. In a medium bowl, sift together the flour, cinnamon, salt, baking soda, and baking powder. 3. In a separate medium bowl, beat together the eggs, sugar, and vegetable oil. Add the dry ingredients to the wet ingredients. Add the courgette and nuts and stir gently until well combined. Transfer the batter to the prepared ramekins or baking pan. 4. Place the ramekins or pan in the air fryer basket. Set the air fryer to 164°C for 15 minutes, or until a cake tester or toothpick inserted into the center comes out clean. If it doesn't, cook for 3 to 5 minutes more and test again. 5. Let cool in the ramekins or pan on a wire rack for 10 minutes. Carefully remove from the ramekins or pan and let cool completely on the rack before serving.

Rhubarb and Strawberry Crumble

Prep time: 10 minutes | Cook time: 12 to 17 minutes | Serves 6

185 g sliced fresh strawberries
15 g sliced rhubarb
40 g granulated sugar
80 g quick-cooking oatmeal
60 g whole-wheat pastry flour, or plain flour
30 g packed light brown sugar
½ teaspoon ground cinnamon
3 tablespoons unsalted butter, melted

1. Insert the crisper plate into the basket and the basket into the unit. Preheat the unit by selecting BAKE, setting the temperature to 192°C, and setting the time to 3 minutes. Select START/STOP to begin. 2. In a 6-by-2-inch round metal baking pan, combine the strawberries, rhubarb, and granulated sugar. 3. In a medium bowl, stir together the oatmeal, flour, brown sugar, and cinnamon. Stir the melted butter into this mixture until crumbly. Sprinkle the crumble mixture over the fruit. 4. Once the unit is preheated, place the pan into the basket. 5. Select BAKE, set the temperature to 192°C, and set the time to 17 minutes. Select START/STOP to begin. 6. After about 12 minutes, check the crumble. If the fruit is bubbling and the topping is golden brown, it is done. If not, resume cooking. 7. When the cooking is complete, serve warm.

Gingerbread

Prep time: 5 minutes | Cook time: 20 minutes | Makes 1 loaf

Cooking spray	⅛ teaspoon salt
125 g plain flour	1 egg
2 tablespoons sugar	60 g molasses or treacle
¾ teaspoon ground ginger	125 ml buttermilk
¼ teaspoon cinnamon	2 tablespoons oil
1 teaspoon baking powder	1 teaspoon pure vanilla extract
½ teaspoon baking soda	

1. Preheat the air fryer to 164ºC. 2. Spray a baking dish lightly with cooking spray. 3. In a medium bowl, mix together all the dry ingredients. 4. In a separate bowl, beat the egg. Add molasses, buttermilk, oil, and vanilla and stir until well mixed. 5. Pour liquid mixture into dry ingredients and stir until well blended. 6. Pour batter into baking dish and bake at 164ºC for 20 minutes or until toothpick inserted in center of loaf comes out clean.

Applesauce and Chocolate Brownies

Prep time: 10 minutes | Cook time: 15 minutes | Serves 8

30 g unsweetened cocoa powder	60 g granulated sugar
30 g plain flour	1 large egg
¼ teaspoon kosher or coarse sea salt	3 tablespoons unsweetened applesauce
½ teaspoons baking powder	30 g miniature semisweet chocolate chips
3 tablespoons unsalted butter, melted	Coarse sea salt, to taste

1. Preheat the air fryer to 148ºC. 2. In a large bowl, whisk together the cocoa powder, flour, salt, and baking powder. 3. In a separate large bowl, combine the butter, granulated sugar, egg, and applesauce, then use a spatula to fold in the cocoa powder mixture and the chocolate chips until well combined. 4. Spray a baking pan with nonstick cooking spray, then pour the mixture into the pan. Place the pan in the air fryer and bake for 15 minutes or until a toothpick comes out clean when inserted in the middle. 5. Remove the brownies from the air fryer, sprinkle some coarse sea salt on top, and allow to cool in the pan on a wire rack for 20 minutes before cutting and serving.

Kentucky Chocolate Nut Pie

Prep time: 20 minutes | Cook time: 25 minutes | Serves 8

2 large eggs, beaten	125 g milk chocolate chips
80 g butter, melted	2 tablespoons bourbon or cranberry juice
125 g sugar	
60 g plain flour	1 (9-inch) unbaked piecrust
185 g coarsely chopped pecans	

1. In a large bowl, stir together the eggs and melted butter. Add the sugar and flour and stir until combined. Stir in the pecans, chocolate chips, and bourbon until well mixed. 2. Using a fork, prick holes in the bottom and sides of the pie crust. Pour the pie filling into the crust. 3. Preheat the air fryer to 176ºC. 4. Cook for 25 minutes, or until a knife inserted into the middle of the pie comes out clean. Let set for 5 minutes before serving.

Cherry Pie

Prep time: 15 minutes | Cook time: 35 minutes | Serves 6

Plain flour, for dusting	1 egg
2 refrigerated piecrusts, at room temperature	1 tablespoon water
	1 tablespoon sugar
1 (355 g) can cherry pie filling	

1. Dust a work surface with flour and place the piecrust on it. Roll out the piecrust. Invert a shallow air fryer baking pan, or your own pie pan that fits inside the air fryer basket, on top of the dough. Trim the dough around the pan, making your cut ½ inch wider than the pan itself. 2. Repeat with the second piecrust but make the cut the same size as or slightly smaller than the pan. 3. Put the larger crust in the bottom of the baking pan. Don't stretch the dough. Gently press it into the pan. 4. Spoon in enough cherry pie filling to fill the crust. Do not overfill. 5. Using a knife or pizza cutter, cut the second piecrust into 1-inch-wide strips. Weave the strips in a lattice pattern over the top of the cherry pie filling. 6. Insert the crisper plate into the basket and the basket into the unit. Preheat the unit by selecting BAKE, setting the temperature to 164ºC, and setting the time to 3 minutes. Select START/STOP to begin. 7. In a small bowl, whisk the egg and water. Gently brush the egg wash over the top of the pie. Sprinkle with the sugar and cover the pie with aluminum foil. 8. Once the unit is preheated, place the pie into the basket. 9. Select BAKE, set the temperature to 164ºC, and set the time to 35 minutes. Select START/STOP to begin. 10. After 30 minutes, remove the foil and resume cooking for 3 to 5 minutes more. The finished pie should have a flaky golden brown crust and bubbling pie filling. 11. When the cooking is complete, serve warm. Refrigerate leftovers for a few days.

Blackberry Peach Cobbler with Vanilla

Prep time: 10 minutes | Cook time: 20 minutes | Serves 4

Filling:	2 tablespoons sunflower oil
170 g blackberries	1 tablespoon maple syrup
185 g chopped peaches, cut into ½-inch thick slices	1 teaspoon vanilla
	3 tablespoons coconut sugar
2 teaspoons arrowroot or cornflour	60 g rolled oats
	40 g whole-wheat pastry flour
2 tablespoons coconut sugar	1 teaspoon cinnamon
1 teaspoon lemon juice	¼ teaspoon nutmeg
Topping:	⅛ teaspoon sea salt

Make the Filling: 1. Combine the blackberries, peaches, arrowroot, coconut sugar, and lemon juice in a baking pan. 2. Using a rubber spatula, stir until well incorporated. Set aside. Make the Topping: 3. Preheat the air fryer to 160ºC 4. Combine the oil, maple syrup, and vanilla in a mixing bowl and stir well. Whisk in the remaining ingredients. Spread this mixture evenly over the filling. 5. Place the pan in the air fryer basket and bake for 20 minutes, or until the topping is crispy and golden brown. Serve warm

Mixed Berries with Pecan Streusel Topping

Prep time: 5 minutes | Cook time: 17 minutes | Serves 3

60 g mixed berries
Cooking spray
Topping:
1 egg, beaten
3 tablespoons almonds, slivered
3 tablespoons chopped pecans
2 tablespoons chopped walnuts
3 tablespoons granulated sweetener
2 tablespoons cold salted butter, cut into pieces
½ teaspoon ground cinnamon

1. Preheat the air fryer to 172ºC. Lightly spray a baking dish with cooking spray. 2. Make the topping: In a medium bowl, stir together the beaten egg, nuts, sweetener, butter, and cinnamon until well blended. 3. Put the mixed berries in the bottom of the baking dish and spread the topping over the top. 4. Bake in the preheated air fryer for 17 minutes, or until the fruit is bubbly and topping is golden brown. 5. Allow to cool for 5 to 10 minutes before serving.

Blueberry-Cream Cheese Bread Pudding

Prep time: 15 minutes | Cook time: 1 hour 10 minutes | Serves 6

125 g light cream
4 large eggs
100 g granulated sugar
1 teaspoon pure lemon extract
500 g cubed croissants (4 to 5 croissants)
125 g blueberries
110 g cream cheese, cut into small cubes

1. In a large bowl, combine the cream, eggs, sugar, and the extract. Whisk until well combined. Add the cubed croissants, blueberries, and cream cheese. Toss gently until everything is thoroughly combined; set aside. 2. Place a 3-cup Bundt pan in the air fryer basket. Preheat the air fryer to 204ºC. 3. Sprinkle the remaining 3 tablespoons sugar in the bottom of the hot pan. Set the air fryer to 204ºC for 10 minutes, or until the sugar caramelises. Tip the pan to spread the caramel evenly across the bottom of the pan. 4. Remove the pan from the air fryer and pour in the bread mixture, distributing it evenly across the pan. Place the pan in the air fryer basket. Set the air fryer to 176ºC for 60 minutes, or until the custard is set in the middle. Let stand for 10 minutes before unmolding onto a serving plate.

Almond Shortbread

Prep time: 10 minutes | Cook time: 12 minutes | Serves 8

125 g unsalted butter
60 g sugar
1 teaspoon pure almond extract
125 g plain flour

1. In bowl of a stand mixer fitted with the paddle attachment, beat the butter and sugar on medium speed until light and fluffy, 3 to 4 minutes. Add the almond extract and beat until combined, about 30 seconds. Turn the mixer to low. Add the flour a little at a time and beat for about 2 minutes more until well-incorporated. 2. Pat the dough into an even layer in a baking pan. Place the pan in the air fryer basket. Set the air fryer to 192ºC for 12 minutes. 3. Carefully remove the pan from air fryer basket. While the shortbread is still warm and soft, cut it into 8 wedges. 4. Let cool in the pan on a wire rack for 5 minutes. Remove the wedges from the pan and let cool completely on the rack before serving.

Apple Fries

Prep time: 10 minutes | Cook time: 7 minutes | Serves 8

Oil, for spraying
125 g plain flour
3 large eggs, beaten
125 g digestive biscuit crumbs
30 g sugar
1 teaspoon ground cinnamon
3 large Gala apples, peeled, cored, and cut into wedges
250 g caramel sauce, warmed

1. Preheat the air fryer to 192ºC. Line the air fryer basket with baking paper and spray lightly with oil. 2. Place the flour and beaten eggs in separate bowls and set aside. In another bowl, mix together the biscuit crumbs, sugar, and cinnamon. 3. Working one at a time, coat the apple wedges in the flour, dip in the egg, and dredge in the biscuit mix until evenly coated. 4. Place the apples in the prepared basket, taking care not to overlap, and spray lightly with oil. You may need to work in batches, depending on the size of your air fryer. 5. Cook for 5 minutes, flip, spray with oil, and cook for another 2 minutes, or until crunchy and golden brown. 6. Drizzle the caramel sauce over the top and serve.

Printed in Great Britain
by Amazon